ALSO BY ALEXANDER ROSE

So You're Going to Be a Witness

PAY
THE
TWO
DOLLARS

or
How to Stay Out of Court
and
What to Do When You Get There
by

ALEXANDER ROSE

Drawings by Paul Coker

SIMON AND SCHUSTER · NEW YORK

FIRST PRINTING

LIBRARY OF CONGRESS CATALOG CARD NUMBER: 57-12395

MANUFACTURED IN THE UNITED STATES OF AMERICA

PRINTED BY REEHL LITHO COMPANY, INC., NEW YORK

BOUND BY H. WOLFF BOOK MFG. CO., INC., NEW YORK

TO CLARA

CONTENTS

PAY
THE
TWO
DOLLARS

1

HOW IT STARTS

ANY MOVE you make, any word you utter, can touch off a lawsuit.

He drives his car like an idiot while you are doing a careful sixty on the right side of the road: boom — ambulance — hospital — lawsuit.

He plays his television at two o'clock in the morning while you are trying to sleep off that office party. You knock on his door to discuss it and find his vocabulary limited to a punch on the nose: fist fight — police station — magistrate's court.

She finds Daisy's other stocking in the suit you gave her to clean: crash — hospital — divorce court.

They come from all directions and want to share in

Uncle Myser's estate: wham — lawyers — papers — surrogate's court.

Subway train . . . Who you pushing? . . . Who is who pushing? . . . Your Honor, this man is a positive maniac . . .

You sign on with the Skinner Paper Hat Company as a salesman. Six months later you are on the witness stand saying, "Your Honor, this Skinner owes me four thousand in commissions. He won't pay. He says they are house accounts. He is an absolute liar. He never heard of these accounts till I brought them in."

You offer your house for sale and one month later find yourself in court listening to this: "Yes, Your Honor, Hookem *is* my real name. I am a real-estate broker. I worked like a dog to bring about this deal and finally got the buyer and seller together on every detail. Then at the last minute this man changed his mind and wouldn't sell. I found out he got more money elsewhere. I claim there was a meeting of the minds . . . "

You fall down a manhole and later find yourself before Judge Fearfle, listening to this:

"Judge, it was his own fault; he must have kicked the cover off with his foot because he was walking sideways to get a better look at this girl's ankle. We know this because when he came out of the ether that's all he kept raving about. The doctor will testify . . . "

You write a book —plagiarism. Invent something — infringement. Send your laundry out — lost. Hire a window cleaner — no parachute. Sit for a portrait — no likeness. Demand overtime pay — no soap.

You buy a loaf of bread and your husband accuses you of attempted murder because there is a piece of glass in the bread and it lacerates his throat. So you sue the baker and allege that maybe he was wearing glasses when he baked the bread and somehow got careless and one of the lenses fell into the dough. But on cross-examination the baker's lawyer burns you to a crisp with this:

Q: Madam, we now know that the baker has never worn glasses in his life, don't we?

A: Well, look here — are you saying that my husband didn't —

Q: I am not talking about your husband. I am talking about the baker. Now, what did you cook for dinner that evening?

A: What do you mean?

Q: What do you think I mean?

THE COURT: He means what did you cook for dinner that evening.

THE WITNESS: Meatballs.

Q: Madam, I see that *you* wear glasses. How long have you worn them?

A: What do you mean how long?

THE COURT: He means how long have you worn glasses.

THE WITNESS: Fifteen years.

Q: Madam, have *you* ever been careless with your glasses? Have you ever dropped them? In fifteen years? Into, say, a pot of *meatballs*?

The lawyer, an old-timer with a rich basso profundo, brings this question to a crashing close with a beautiful crescendo, and as the thunder reverberates through the courtroom the judge leans forward to regard you more closely, the jurors cock their heads, the spectators fidget, and even your husband, who doesn't wear glasses, sizes you up as if he sees you for the first time. At which point you are pretty close to a heart condition and may not even make it to the door.

If you are a housewife and hire a girl to do a little

3

part-time dusting and she breaks a leg tripping over that roller skate belonging to the apple of your eye, you may owe her a lot of money. If, in addition, her mad leap across the living-room floor ends up in the corner, where this apple's brother left the iron fire engine, and she sustains a fractured skull, you may owe this girl so much you might have to go out yourself and do a stretch of full-time dusting to pay it off.

Or your nine-year-old boy throws a playmate through a plate-glass window, and you get a letter from the store owner, who hates children, demanding $340 for the shattered window and $612.13 for ruined merchandise. Even if your boy says he was defending himself from two hoodlums, he will have to *prove* it, and will he make a good witness? And will you be able to cover up that episode with the baseball bat in the schoolyard and the Halloween thing with the lead pipe? You might have to get rid of the boy or cut down his calories.

You might try a round of golf to forget your troubles and not know your own strength and drive the ball smack into the right eye of a citizen. The way things are going, it might be just your luck that he already has a glass eye and this about does it. There might be a lot of money involved here, especially if he is a scientist and needs his eye to look through the microscope. Will you be a good witness? Or will you blurt? Surely you won't say, "Your Honor, of all the people I have hit in my time, this man was hurt the least; I think he is exaggerating."

You might try to get away from it all, get the car out of the garage somehow and go for a spin, and on the way meet your best friend. You say, "Get in, Marge." She does, and you close the door — on her finger. Friend or not, she sues you for five thousand dollars. Remember, she plays the piano in a night club and you are trying to put her out of work.

4

Suppose you are a dentist. You can be sued for pulling the wrong tooth, pulling it too hard or too fast. All this, mind you, while another patient is taking a header on the wet floor of your reception room (because of your sloppy maid) and wondering what it is worth.

Perhaps you are a surgeon and take pride not only in your skill but in your neatness. Suddenly comes the paper demanding fifty thousand dollars. Remember that pair of scissors you thought the nurse took home for her personal use? Well, she didn't do it and you owe her an apology, because this patient says he has been carrying it around in his abdomen for five months. Naturally you are glad to get the scissors back — but fifty thousand dollars!

You might be just a next-door neighbor, having a drink with a friend in Apartment 4M as he attempts to set up the expensive hi-fi layout he got for Christmas. You watch his childish efforts as long as you can and then say, "Joe, for Pete's sake, that's not kid's work. You sit over here and relax; I'll have this going in no time."

So you blow out all the tubes, connect the wrong wires, scratch up the records, and damn near put the house on fire, ruining the hi-fi outfit beyond repair. Joe sues you for twenty-eight hundred dollars, which fortunately includes the damage to the oil painting of his wife when she was younger and wore bangs.

When you get the summons for twenty-eight hundred dollars you feel it is an outrage because you meant well, and besides, you didn't do it for pay and you are not even in the electrical business; you handle pickles. But the law says you owe the money because you undertook to make the installation, and when you do that you must do it right or suffer the consequences. You resolve never to tie a friend's bow tie, but that is small comfort.

Leave something out of a contract, put a wrong word in a receipt, pay a debt in cash, make a wrong move, and there you are, your left hand on the Book, your right hand aloft, staring into a sea of strange faces and wondering if you'll ever make it.

2

WHEN YOU ARE
THE DEFENDANT

A TYPICAL CASE

THE MAN SAYS politely, "Are you Mr. Trembal, sir?"

You nod genially. "The very same. And what can I do for you, sir?"

"I have a paper for you," says the man, handing it over and gliding out.

You unfold it with the practiced flair of a solid executive, do a double-take and nearly drop dead.

"Hey," you yell, catching the man at the elevator, "this is a summons!" He nods and presses the button. You sputter, "This is a summons-and-complaint!" He nods and jabs the button again. You explode: "For twenty-five

7

thousand dollars! Somebody is suing me for twenty-five thousand dollars! This is crazy! Why, I never — I don't even know this — Hey, wait a minute!" Your wheels are working. Yes, it is the very same: a year ago, almost to the day, that little Austin you sideswiped on the highway. Now it's all coming back: the small, bespectacled scold creeping out of that preposterous scooter and giving you the dressing down of your life, over a slightly dented fender; the brief exchange of license information and — you can see him clearly, striding briskly back to his flea box and disappearing in a cloud of dust. There wasn't a mark on him, or a displaced thread of lint, and as for the four-wheeled sardine can, two dollars' worth of work would have repaired the dent and given the mechanic a fat profit.

You scan the papers again. The little monster claims twenty-five thousand dollars, and breaks it down this way: $792.36 for damage to the car; $102.12 for rental of another car during the repair; $206.94 for damage to a pair of expensive binoculars that was lying on the front seat; $416.21 for damage to an imported Italian accordion that was resting on the rear seat; repair of a blue serge suit, $19.10; medical expenses, $316.25; and $23,147.02 for pain and suffering.

Your first thought is of some monstrous typographical error, but the man still waiting for the elevator seems to read your thought and shakes his head. Your next thought is of the District Attorney, the Police Department, and finally the FBI.

You spend the rest of the day muttering about how fantastic this all is: a dented fender, the plaintiff leaving the scene as sound as a dollar, and a lawsuit for twenty-five thousand dollars, which even in this day and age is more than somewhat.

Now, it is true that this Austin character is laying it on thick and will certainly not get away with that kind of money in a court of law. But how much of it *will* he get away with? Suppose that shortly after this thing with the fender he ran into a brick wall — he looked the type — and acquired some real injuries? And as for the binoculars and the accordion, they *might* have been in the car. He can also produce a doctor, who treated him for the actual injuries, and a whopping mechanic's bill. If the doctor's and the mechanic's bills stand up, his claim for pain and suffering begins to look pretty good and you begin to get pretty sick about the whole thing.

Oh, yes, you are insured, but do you carry enough? Even you know that the insurance company is liable only to the extent of your coverage and that anything over that must come out of your pocket; so that if your policy covers you up to ten thousand dollars and this . . . this plaintiff gets a verdict for twenty-five thousand, you are ready for the man with the white coat.

You could have avoided this whole terrible mess by taking a few simple measures at the time of the occurrence, which brings us to the threshold of our next section:

HOW TO ANTICIPATE A LAWSUIT

THE TWO important things about a lawsuit are: 1. Who was at fault? 2. What were the actual damages?

The thing to do *as quickly as possible* is to try to pinpoint the amount or extent of the damages in some way — that is, try to get some kind of admission from the party who is likely to sue as to what he claims the damages are.

It is important that this be done as soon after the occurrence as possible, so that the party doesn't have time

9

to consult with his omniscient brother-in-law, or check with his wife's furrier as to the price of a new mink, or check your rating to see what you will go for.

Very often this important information is easy to nail down, yet nearly always it is overlooked by the layman, who believes the big thing to establish is the liability, or who was at fault. It is, of course, the big thing, but not *at this point*.

It can be done this way: You are driving along. The madman in front stops short. You dent his fender — about sixty cents' worth. You both get out screaming. You exchange licenses and look things over. Now here it is: Even if you feel that you are not at fault, that he is entirely to blame, *don't let him go* until you have both thoroughly inspected the vehicles. If you can persuade him to jot down his damages on a piece of paper — fine! If not, ask the nearest person to have a look, and get the person's name. You can tell him readily you are not asking him to fix any blame but merely to observe the extent of the damage.

Once you have obtained some scrap of evidence concerning the extent of the damage, you eliminate the possibility of some enormous and ridiculous claim and you can fight out the question of who is to blame with some degree of calm.

If you had let him go without pinning him down to his damages, he might later decide you could go for a carbon and valve job, new brake linings, a master cylinder, a new transmission and a paint job. And a damaged Stradivarius. This has been successfully done ever since the invention of the wheel.

It would also be well to have him say no one was injured. If you don't, you may be horrified later to learn that he claims to be sick, sore, lame and disabled, due to the severe brain concussion and sacroiliac sprain caused by your carelessness — twenty-five thousand dollars' worth.

It is true he can still claim that all these infirmities developed after he got home, and during the week, but his story will have rough going in the face of that little memo you have — in his own handwriting — or that by-stander's testimony, which would prove conclusively that a trivial fender dent could never have resulted in such injuries.

Now, if he refuses to play this little game, if he says, "Look, buddy, I haven't time to give you my life story; you got my number," and if no bystander is willing to look at the alleged damages, your next move is to call a policeman or ask the bystander to call one while you stick to your man. (He will do this. Everybody loves to call a policeman; something to do with Freud.)

When this worthy arrives you may be disconcerted to find the thing going like this:

"What's goin' on here?"

"Officer, we've just had a little — "

"You got this party's number?"

"Yes, but — "

"Then on your way. You're blockin' traffic."

"But, Officer, I want someone to have a look at the damage."

"Is that what you called me for?"

"Exactly. You see, sir — "

"Look, mister, I ought to pull you in. I'll bet you're one of them taxpayers says we ought to be out chasing thieves. You got this party's number. What more do you want? Now, get them vehicles outa here, the both of you."

Well, the officer has a point there, but if you can keep your shirt on and get him to understand that you are merely trying to prevent an unwarranted claim for prop-

11

erty damage or personal injury, he may at least look the situation over, however briefly. Then you can subpoena him at the trial and even his reluctant testimony will help a lot to defeat an outlandish claim.

It goes without saying that if a couple of people actually saw the accident and were willing to testify, you would be in great luck. However, most people are reluctant to become involved, since court appearances take up a great deal of time and the rigors of cross-examination are a great pain, so it is well to bring away from the scene as much detail as you possibly can. The time of day, the condition of the weather, the color of the signal lights, distances from one point to another, the make, year and condition of the cars — the condition of the drivers too — and who was at the wheel at the time of the occurrence — all of this information will be of inestimable help to your lawyer in preparing your defense and defeating an unwarranted or exaggerated claim.

The last item — who was at the wheel — needs an additional word. Not infrequently an unauthorized person — that is, a person without a license — is at the wheel of a car and has probably caused the accident. On the heels of the impact a friend who has a license slips behind the wheel — a little matter usually unnoticed in the excitement — and then in court swears that *he* was driving.

Everyone has heard the expression "Me and my big mouth." This is not from the Latin or Greek. It means about what it says, and the point is: Be careful (remember you are a prospective defendant) not to blurt out any damaging admissions or make any careless remarks right after an accident or other occurrence. It is amazing how a little word or a phrase is remembered long afterward, and you wind up on the witness stand coping with this:

12

Q: Mr. Blert, if you didn't cause the whole thing, why did you say you were sorry?

A: What!

Q: Why did you say you were sorry?

A: Sorry?

Q: Sorry.

A: Good heavens, the man was bleeding and I simply said —

Q: Were you sorry about his bleeding or about your *carelessness?*

A: Carelessness! Why, he was driving with his arm around this girl! How could *I* be careless?

Q: It's possible. Now, did you also say that the lights were dim and —

A: Look here, sir —

Whether you finally win this verbal brawl or not, it won't be comfortable and could have been avoided if you had made no unnecessary remarks at the scene.

DEFENSES

DEFENSES, IN both civil and criminal cases, do not vary as much as you might think.

If a man is being sued and does not wish to pay the claim, he must make some explanation in court about the matter. If a man is charged with a crime and does not wish to go to jail, he must explain the thing somehow.

Brown is suing Jones. Another automobile collision. Brown says that he was driving carefully, minding his own business, when suddenly Jones crashed into the rear of his car, inflicting the usual injuries and then some.

13

Brown is asking fifteen thousand dollars. What can Jones possibly say by way of defense to this claim?

Well, he could say he was out of town at the time. But of course not; Brown has his license number and witnesses.

He could deny that Brown was injured, but that is out because Brown still has the scars and will bring a doctor to court to prove the treatment; and there is the ambulance report, and the police officer's testimony.

So things look bad for Jones, because nobody likes a man who will hit anybody in the rear. Jones needs a defense, because actually the way it happened was that he suddenly got an eyeful of this unbelievable creature with the incredible measurements weaving her way along the sidewalk, his head did a 135-degree swivel and his

foot nearly drove the gas pedal through the floor-board, which is not the best way to stop a car.

There is really only one defense available to Jones, which happens to be the most popular in this sort of situation: He can say that Brown stopped short.

Yes, he hit Brown. Yes, in the rear. Yes, the injuries are bad.

But Brown stopped short.

This is a very popular defense, perhaps because it happens to be the actual cause of many accidents.

This defense has more of a chance than might seem possible and about all that poor Brown can do about it when he hears it for the first time is turn purple and protest to the heavens — unless an eyewitness actually saw the thing happen.

Incidentally, just at this point we can see how very important any kind of remark made *at the scene* actually is. If Jones makes no mention of this short-stop business *right away,* this whole defense is out the window. Look:

Q: Mr. Jones, you say Brown stopped short?
A: He sure did.
Q: And yet at the time you made no mention of it?
A: Well, I didn't want —
Q: Continue.
A: That is to say, the whole —
Q: Please finish.
A: He knew —
Q: He knew what?
A: Well, he knew he stopped short. Why should *I* tell him?

Right here don't bet on Jones, because it is obvious even to the jurors that he thought up this short-stop defense on his way home.

But look here, you don't just walk into court and say, "Yes, I did it. Where do I pay?" Jones still needs a defense.

How about saying Brown backed up!

Ridiculous. Who backs up on a crowded highway — and what on earth for? Sheer nonsense.

Wait! Maybe Brown was driving one of those new foreign cars, where you get in backwards, and wasn't sure which —

Come, this is no time for joking.

15

No; about all Jones can do with this thing is try to settle it, and we will see how he does that a little later on.

HEAD-ON COLLISION

THIS ONE is dreadful. Smith is suing Clayton. Head-on collision. Smith claims he was driving along on the proper side of the street, when Clayton suddenly came over to the *wrong* side (wrong for Clayton), smashed his headlights for a starter, practically killed him, and broke his watch. This lawsuit is also for thousands.

Clayton needs a defense as badly as Jones did, if not more so, because he went over to the wrong side of the street to hit Smith.

A flagrant violation such as this often inspires a brilliant defense, probably because that is the only kind of a defense that will work. So Clayton says that a child suddenly ran across his path, and he swerved to avoid striking the child; that the accident was unavoidable; that he used his best judgment in an emergency and is not to be blamed. In fact, he feels sorry about Smith's headlights.

Where is the child? Well, that is the big question. If Clayton could produce the child he would have no problem. If he could produce a witness who saw the child around the scene either before or after the crash — if he could produce someone who saw *a* child — it might lend some credence to his story. But if there is no trace of a child in this picture, it will be a pure question of how convincing a witness Clayton makes on the stand with this story, because the lawyer for Smith will say something like this on summation:

Ladies and gentlemen of the jury; I do not know how

16

many of you have heard this kind of a defense before, the one about the child-dashing-in-front-of-the-car, but it is an old one. It is about the only defense possible, I suppose, to explain this flagrant disregard for human life, this wanton carelessness on the part of Clayton. If I may add a word to an old and true saying: Children should be seen and not heard about! Produce that child, I say . . .

There are a number of variations of this type of defense which, as the lawyer says, is about the only type of defense that could explain an open-and-shut violation on the part of a defendant. There is the child who appeared suddenly out of thin air from behind a parked car, chasing a rubber ball; there is the dog dashing across the path,

chasing whatever dogs chase; there is the sudden, foot-deep hole in the road to be avoided; and so on.

Again, the importance of remarks made at the scene cannot be overstressed, for the defense must tie in with any such remarks (or lack of them) , because after the smoke has cleared away and you are down at the lawyer's office planning your defense you may find that some beautiful story is not available to you because you did (or didn't) say something at the scene that will help the story stand up in court.

That is why, unless you can think clearly in a climate of excitement and emotion and have at least a smattering of legal hocus-pocus, it is better not to talk too much.

THE COUNTERCLAIM

THERE ARE times when a man has absolutely no defense to a lawsuit. This is a horrible position to be in, especially in a case involving a very large sum of money. Such a man is really sitting on the horns of a dilemma, which is even worse than a posture chair.

This man is not without hope, because there is always the counterclaim.

The counterclaim is very popular, and it should be, because it is very handy.

If somebody sues you and you have no defense, not even duress, you *could* have a counterclaim. You could say:

Yes, I owe Dewars a thousand dollars on that promissory note, but he seems to forget that he owes me eleven hundred for services that I performed at various times. What services? Why, he came to me for advice from time to time. Seems he was in love with a young, attractive widow who was driving him crazy. Every time they had words and she wouldn't speak to him, he came running to me for advice and I would straighten him out. Sometimes it took a couple of hours for one conference. He came hundreds of times. I figure two dollars a conference and cheap at that. He

18

got some pretty sound advice. That widow finally ran off with a banker and took the banker for all he had.

While this particular counterclaim is not strictly from the files, there are a number of actual counterclaims that can be cited.

In one of the small-claims courts of Portland a lady sued a barber for $4.50. He was no ordinary barber, for the lady said he sold all sorts of odds and ends and was active in many different directions. She claimed he sold her a contraceptive device which turned out to be defective. She wanted her money back, $4.50.

The barber not only denied this claim but had a counterclaim: he was a piccolo teacher on the side, and the lady owed him five dollars for piccolo lessons.

Both claims were finally thrown out and the barber moved to another location.

In a Southern state a father sued his son for $5,000. The father claimed he had spent that sum on the boy's medical education, and now that the boy was a full-fledged doctor with a good practice, it should be repaid. He said the son had promised, from time to time, that he would repay every penny of this money.

But in court the son had a counterclaim. His father had been ill for a long time and he, the doctor-son, had treated him — diathermy treatments by the hundred, and baking and massage and so on, and the medical bill totaled more than $5,000, but he was willing to settle his counterclaim for $5,000.

From these facts, it is doubtful whether anybody could possibly like this doctor-son, but let us see what was really back of this screwy lawsuit:

Soon after hanging out his shingle the doctor began to support his father, giving him as much money as he could spare. Presently, as the doctor's practice grew, a horde of relatives descended upon him and gathered up every odd two-bit piece they found lying about. They got him for small loans and large loans; they put themselves in business with his money. And the family was large and had many children and the doctor was called out of his bed at all hours to dash about treating these children for ailments real and imaginary. And the children had parents who were a sickly lot.

But the doctor was a good-natured fellow and he never complained.

Then the doctor got married.

And the fun began. The doctor's wife put her foot down. Enough was enough. It was all right to support the father. But not like a playboy. Besides, what about the other brothers who were all in business and doing well — all four of them? Why didn't they contribute? And those neurotic relatives and their children — what was this anyway, a clinic?

20

The doctor was fond of his wife, and the first thing you knew he was a changed man. Then the relatives got hold of the father and talked to him.

These talks resulted in a lawsuit, and it was quite evident the father's heart was not really in it. It was equally evident the son didn't like his own counterclaim either.

So the judge called all the parties to his chambers and, after an arduous job of work, settled the matter to the satisfaction of everyone. Except the relatives.

Counterclaims must be pretty good to stand up. Usually a counterclaim has a tendency to lift the eyebrow because it isn't alleged until the original claim is brought. In the father-and-son case above, a juror might well reason: Why did this doctor wait until his father sued him before making a claim for those alleged treatments? If he were really in earnest about wanting to be paid for them, he would have brought suit against the father and the father would have had to bring the counterclaim.

However, if a counterclaim is not too far-fetched, and if the delay in bringing it out can be explained, it can be quite helpful.

HOW TO WIN A LAWSUIT BEFORE IT STARTS

So YOU'RE going to build!

Well, as your British cousin would say: Mind your step. The thing to look out for is not the falling timber, the flying bricks, the shaky scaffolding, the loose gratings, the cracked plaster. These are as nothing. They can only hit you on the head or throw you on your face or land you on your ear and send you to the hospital. Trifles!

21

The things to look out for are the Extras. The extras will not only send you to the hospital; they will keep you there.

The contract says you get *everything* for fifteen thousand dollars. But after you have paid out the fifteen thousand and the job is about fifty per cent under way — that is, the castle of your dreams is one big, hopeless pile of rubble — all work stops, the men walk off, your wife is at her mother's under the doctor's care and you are in court defending a mechanic's lien action. The contractor is on the stand, being questioned by his own lawyer:

Q: Tell us about it, Mr. Graab.

A: Well, we were going along fine, according to schedule. We had the roof up, the floors laid down, all the plumbing and electrical work installed. Then Mr. Spendor came down. It was on a Tuesday, and his wife was with him.

She took one look at the closets and said, "Not enough closets!" Just like that. I said, "Madam, if you will just look at the blueprints — " She stopped me dead. She said, "These closets will have to go; they are all

22

too small and there are not enough of them. I want four more."

I said, "Madam, in that case this stairway will have to come down, and if you do that all the walls on the second floor — "

After three weeks of detailed testimony it develops that you owe the contractor $9,612.13 more, and you will have to do without copper leaders, unless you want to make a new contract and leave out the stairs.

So that it is most important so to word the contract that even the slightest change, addition or alteration will be in writing and that no claim will be valid unless it is initialed by both the owner and the contractor. In other words, have the contract so worded that no oral change will be permitted.

There is one fly in the ointment here and he is bigger than an elephant: The law and its interpretation by judicial scholars is so complex that even a contract which forbids an oral change may be changed orally. Fasten your seat belt and look at this very recent decision of the Appellate Division in New York: The proprietor of a store was seeking an injunction and damages in a certain situation, the facts of which we need not bother with for the moment. In the Appellate Division he argued that even if he had made the oral modification it was invalid because his lease prohibited such a verbal change. Now:

The Appellate Division disregarded this contention, quoting Judge Cardozo to the effect that "those who make a contract may unmake it. The clause which forbids a change may be changed like any other. The prohibition of oral waiver may itself be waived."

So, as the fellow says, there you are.

But a ray of hope pierces the fog. You can take a giant

step toward protecting yourself: Whenever you go into a deal that is going to stretch out over a period of time — whether it is building a house, decorating an apartment, writing an opera or whatever — buy a ten-cent notebook and from the first day on keep a careful, daily record of conversations, dates, amounts and other pertinent data.

In this way you will be ready for the most outlandish claims upon your pocketbook, and when the fellow is on the stand testifying like mad about things that never happened, you can be tugging at your lawyer's sleeve and whispering, *"Impossible. Couldn't have happened. He didn't see Bleery until the 25th because Bleery and I weren't bailed out until the 24th. Here it is — all here!"*

In addition to this daily diary, set up a folder, and from the first day on put into it every slip of paper, invoice, receipt, letter and envelope connected with the project. You will be astonished in a very short time to find that you can hardly lift this folder and then be very grateful that you don't have to go looking for these things when you need them.

To recapitulate: It is not quite enough to be honest and truthful; it is necessary to *prove* these qualities in the courtroom, and any scrap of paper or neatly kept record that will help you do this is money in the bank.

CIRCUMSTANTIAL EVIDENCE

IF YOU ARE a pickpocket and you are arrested at the exact instant that your working hand is deep in a stranger's pocket, it is a comfort to know that at least you have been convicted on *direct* evidence and not *circumstantial* evidence.

From the facts just stated, it is not necessary for the

jury to infer *other* facts necessary to send you away for a spell; the facts are there, plain for all to see, and it is an open-and-shut, red-handed, dead-to-rights deal.

But let us say that you are still a pickpocket, dangling from a strap on an uptown bus, humming softly, minding your own business — and doing very well at it — and suddenly a stranger roars, "I've been robbed!"

The bus driver swivels around sharply. He spots you gazing innocently out the window. He shouts, "If it isn't Louie!" and signals to a passing police officer, who jumps aboard the bus and gathers you up.

Now you will be convicted on *circumstantial* evidence because:

1. You are a celebrated pickpocket and have been in practice for many years.
2. The stranger's money and papers are missing — definitely.
3. You were standing next to him.
4. Part of his blue serge suit is under your fingernails — with a pin stripe.
5. Your last four arrests were on buses — all going uptown.
6. You always hum the same tune after a job.
7. You didn't have time to get rid of the leather and it is on you, with the money and paper intact.
8. You also have his watch — monogramed.

Now, it may be that you can explain these items away, but in case you can't, it is nice to know that they are circumstantial evidence; in other words, no one actually saw you pull this caper, but there are enough facts to infer that you *did,* and you thereby become a victim of circumstantial evidence.

You don't even have to be a celebrated pickpocket.

25

Even an ordinary citizen is not safe from this kind of evidence.

Suppose you are walking down the street at three o'clock in the morning. Silence reigns; not a soul is abroad. Suddenly shots ring out and a body comes hurtling out of a roaring automobile, with a smoking revolver thrown after it.

There you are on the sidewalk, inspecting the dead man, with the smoking revolver in your hand. Along comes a citizen who grabs you. Other citizens appear and they turn you over to the police.

You are either in an awful jam, or you have nothing to worry about — depending upon a number of things.

If you are a businessman, manufacturing musical salt- and pepper-shakers, and you were walking along that street because it is the route you always take from the railroad station to your home around the corner, and it was three o'clock in the morning because you were taking inventory and the work sheets are in your pocket, and you never saw the dead man in your life — you have nothing

26

to worry about, because that cluster of facts does not make you look like a murderer.

But if you are out of work and if you were walking along that street because it wasn't some other street, and it was three o'clock in the morning because it wasn't earlier, and you also served a short stretch three years ago for housebreaking — you are in an awful jam, because that string of facts makes you look like a murderer.

If you are the businessman, one little thing could put you back on the spot: knowing the dead man. If you knew him you will have to explain how — whether it was because he was a neighbor and nothing else; whether you ever had a business transaction with him; whether he ever took your wife out on a date; whether he ever cheated you at cards. If any of these things are true, your musical salt-and pepper-shakers and inventory sheets may not pull you through; your story needs work. You may have to go to church, pay your income taxes, have six children, support your mother and be a teetotaler.

If you are the housebreaker, one little thing may save you: the dead man may not be dead after all.

So . . . neither of these citizens did the killing, but these are their positions in the eyes of the law. The law doesn't know who fired the shots and must take the facts as they seem, in the absence of positive evidence to the contrary.

WATT SHOT ME

A RECENT murder trial was based entirely on circumstantial evidence. A Mrs. Brown had a small store in a small town. One fine day her son, who was a truck driver,

27

stopped his truck outside the store, came in and said, "Mom, I'm going in the back room for a minute." She was busy with customers for some time.

Suddenly two shots rang out. The horrified woman rushed into the back room and found her son slumped down on a davenport, with two gunshot wounds in his chest. There was no one else in the room, there was no gun in view. The only other door in the room was one that opened onto a side street.

She called the police and they took her and her son to the hospital. When the doctors told the police the man was dying, the police had the mother speak to him and ask him who had shot him. He said, "Watt shot me," and died.

A Gordon Watt was promptly picked up by the police. They interrogated him and found that he knew the deceased, that they had quarreled over Watt's attentions to Brown's wife, and Watt admitted having been within one block of the scene of the shooting at the time it occurred.

He was indicted and tried for murder.

The most ambitious district attorney would have been delighted with a package like this, because the circumstantial evidence was beautiful.

BUT —

THE DEFENSE was that the deceased had committed suicide. At the trial, most of the evidence to support this contention was developed from the police officers and detectives who were the State's witnesses.

The door that led to the side street was *locked* when the mother entered the room.

28

The revolver which had been used was found shoved down behind the seat cushions of the davenport. The coronor's physician testified that it would have been possible for the deceased, who was somewhat intoxicated, to have shot himself twice and placed the revolver where it was found.

The dead man's wife said that when he left for work that morning he said, "Ralph made thirty-six, but I won't make thirty." This cryptic remark she interpreted to mean that the deceased, who was twenty-nine, did not expect to live to be thirty, although his brother had lived to be thirty-six.

In the pocket of the jacket that the deceased was wearing was a note, written in pencil on one of his order blanks, reading: "Dear Mom: I am sorry if what I am going to do brings you any grief."

The defendant was acquitted.

But, looking back at his position when he was arrested, it was most uncomfortable. Circumstantial evidence put him into it, but also got him out. Even the dying declaration, "Watt shot me," which would normally be very strong, was overcome, not only by the evidence to the contrary, but by an interesting contention of Watt: that the dying man was actually saying, "What shot me?"

WHAT'S GOING ON?

PEOPLE ARE very careless about putting themselves into positions of danger and trouble, rushing pell-mell into situations from which it will be difficult to break away. A crowd gathers — instantly people rush to the scene to make sure nothing is happening that they ought to know about. Bullets may be flying, a mad dog may be loose, a murderer

29

with a knife, a wife on the rampage — a crowd spells trouble, and it is a good thing to stay away from.

Ringing alarms, talking to drunks, lingering in automobiles at the scene of an accident — all these things should be done with extreme caution, lest you find yourself on the wrong end of a habeas corpus. If you're near enough to the trouble, you may have to do some explaining. If you *must* look over a drunk lying in a doorway, do it with another citizen or passerby so people won't think you're up to your old tricks. Every citizen is innocent until he is proven guilty. But remember that circumstantial evidence is *proof,* if it is strong enough.

Family background, personal character, employment status, marital condition, personal appearance, school record, reputation among friends and associates — all these are important factors in offsetting adverse circumstantial evidence and they will come to your aid when you need them, like the good old cavalry with bugles blowing.

This is probably as it should be, for while circumstantial evidence may seem a harsh thing to go by, it is often the only thing the law has before it, and it usually works out fairly for all.

If a man has led a clean life, if he has taken the trouble to get married and raise a family, if he meets his obligations and is well regarded, why shouldn't these things help him in a dark hour?

If, on the other hand, a man is a bum, if he shirks the responsibility of marriage and the family life, if he is a dead beat and a grouch, many would say it is only fitting that circumstantial evidence should sneak up on him.

True, a man might be out of employment because he cannot get work, he might be without a wife because he is out of shape and has no money, and he might be a grouch because of this, and he might have a poor reputation because of the grouch. Perhaps he can prove these things to a jury. If he cannot, he will have to be patient and see if he can't get a better break in the next world.

THE ALIBI

A VERY HANDY thing. It proves you couldn't have done it.

A man whose wife is a nag might find himself driving along in plenty of time to get home for dinner, about which his wife is very strict.

Suddenly he gets a flat tire.

Now, who is going to believe that? That story is older than the sick friend.

But if our man can locate a policeman, engage him in a word or two of small talk while fixing the flat, and quietly take note of his shield number, he can face his wife with head up and shoulders back, no matter what time he gets home.

At 9 P.M. when she is facing him head-on at the door he can say:

"Now look here, Martha, I don't expect you to believe

31

this, but I had a flat on the road — Martha! Put that thing down, that's a cleaver! You'll kill somebody with that! Now, about this flat. They didn't make me vice-president of the company for nothing, you know; it's because I don't use my noggin for a hatrack, that's why! Now you just pick up that telephone and call the 47th Precinct. Ask for Patrolman No. 1342. Ask him what he saw on the roadway at six o'clock!"

This is a pretty fair alibi, though not guaranteed to work with all wives. A wife who is not husband-minded might see a spot of collusion here and figure the policeman was a barmate of the husband.

With this kind of a wife there is only one alternative for the husband. It is an heroic measure, but it makes the alibi foolproof: While fixing the flat he must engage the officer in a fist fight. This will get him arrested and create official records and even a wife can't beat official records.

An alibi can be established in a number of ways. A disinterested witness is a good form of proof.

Suppose your name is Jones and you are on trial for robbery in the first degree. They say that you robbed the bank at two o'clock in the morning.

But the bank is in Chicago, and your lawyer puts a witness on the stand to prove you couldn't have done it:

Q: What is your occupation, sir?
A: I am a hotel clerk.
Q: What hotel, please?
A: The Intermittent Rest in St. Louis, Mo.
Q: You have just come from St. Louis at my request?
A: Yes, sir.
Q: Now, tell us how you know Jones here.
A: Well, it was rather odd. I was standing behind the hotel desk on the day in question, when a disheveled,

badly banged-up individual approached the desk and said, "Quick, get me up to Room 302." I said, "I am sorry, sir, but a Mr. Jones occupies Room 302 and he has left word that he doesn't wish to be disturbed." Whereupon this mangled-up individual muttered, "Of course, you idiot, of course. I'm Jones. I just fell out of the window." Very odd, I thought.

Q: And it was this Jones, right here at the table?
A: The very same.
Q: And this took place in St. Louis?
A: Yes, sir.
Q: Three hundred miles from Chicago?
A: That's right.
Q: On the very day in question?
A: Yes, sir.

This is a good alibi. It certainly proves you couldn't have held up that bank if you had wanted to.

Unless the hotel clerk is your brother-in-law.

HOW DO YOU PLEAD?

If you drive a car you may get a summons for a traffic violation and have to make a momentous decision — plead Guilty or Not Guilty.

If you live in a big city — New York, say — you have a serious problem, because every moving violation (infraction of the law while the car is in motion) is endorsed on your driver's license, and after a certain number of them, your license is taken away, and you become the sorriest thing in creation: an American without a car.

On top of this, there is a persistent rumor that when each platoon of New York policemen leaves the station-house in the morning, each man equipped with a batch of these summonses, the lieutenant shouts, "Last one to get rid of his summonses is a rotten egg."

While this rumor is unconfirmed, the police do give them away like crazy, and this creates the problem, especially when you are not guilty.

Now, you are riding north on Broadway, say, and the light is green. As you approach Sixty-seventh Street the light changes suddenly to red. You are eight feet from the corner when this happens.

Should you stop or go ahead? You decide you cannot stop with safety, and continue across.

Those noises in your ears are not from last night's wingding at Harry's. They are a police siren.

Now, you know that once the officer starts writing, all is lost; the first little mark on the summons is irrevocable, so you talk fast.

"Now, Officer — "

"License."

"Here you are, sir. Now, Officer — "

"Hmm. I see this is your specialty, passing the lights. . . . Oh, just a minute, friend, I see I'm not spelling your name right; let me fix this M . . . there! Mudd, isn't it?"

"Now, Officer — "

"Here you are, pal, license, registration, summons. That's for the 24th, 9 A.M. Don't lose it, now."

"Now, Officer —"

"Well, so long, pal. Guess we won't see you around after the 24th. Your third one, you know."

Not realizing the officer is gone, you sputter furiously about the injustice of it and are fit to be tied. Later, you are going over it with friends:

FRANK: I say pay the two dollars, Jim.

GEORGE: It's fifteen now.

FRANK: That's an expression. It means don't make a federal case out of it.

PAUL: He's right. Plead "Guilty with an explanation."

YOU: What good will that do?

PAUL: Save you maybe five.

YOU: But that's not the point —

PAUL: There's a point?

YOU: Don't you *understand?* Pleading guilty is the same as a conviction. Says so on the summons. Then it goes on the license, and that's *it.* No car. My wife — have you ever met my wife?

PAUL: You're in trouble.

TOM: He's *not* in trouble. Now hear this —

GEORGE: Sh . . . Tom's an engineer — trouble shooter at the plant; knows everything.

TOM: How fast were you going?

YOU: Slow. About fifteen miles an hour.

TOM: At fifteen miles an hour you need thirty-one and a half feet to stop your car. Matter of fact, sixteen feet of that is reaction time alone — the time it takes for your foot to get the message from your brain to stop the car. Now, you only had eight feet to do all this. Impossible, and that's a perfect defense. You plead Not Guilty.

JERRY: That's beautiful, Tom! But I pleaded Not Guilty once. Did you ever see the traffic courtroom? The place is jammed to the rafters, the judge looks like a worried bookie and he's pushing those cases along like he's late for the last race. Jim will never get a chance to say all that.

FRANK: He has a right to!

JERRY: I have a right to be president.

PAUL: What can he do?

JERRY: He can shoot himself.

GEORGE: That's ridiculous.

JERRY: You ever meet his wife?

TOM: Wait a minute. Jim, listen; you just go down there and *insist* on being heard. You're a citizen, a *United States* citizen, by the gods. Go down there and talk up like one! Let them drag you away while you're doing it, but you talk up till you've had your say! I don't care *who* the judge is, he'll listen, especially if there's maybe a reporter or two around.

JERRY: Tom, that's beautiful! And he *will* listen. But do you know what happens when you *make* a judge listen? It will then be Jim's word against the cop's. Now, the judge has some rights too, you know. He has a right to believe either one. How about that?

PAUL: What can Jim do?

JERRY: He can leave town. Or he can get a good pair of stout shoes for walking. Town shoes. I had a pair of shoes once —

It is a serious problem, and only the man who gets the summons can decide whether he wants to spend two or three hours or a couple of days in a crowded courtroom waiting for his case to be called, on the chance of being acquitted. Perhaps policemen should be vested with a little more discretion in handing out these summonses, since they are right on the scene and in the best position to appraise the merits of the matter, so that if there is a probable doubt about the violation it might be resolved with a warning and save everyone a lot of time and money.

One irate citizen recently blew his top about this and went further than all the way. He received a summons for parking overtime at a parking meter. When he explained to the policeman at the scene that the meter was defective, the policeman listened politely — while writing the ticket.

The citizen pleaded not guilty. He spent two full days in court and was finally found not guilty, when the policeman admitted that the meter was defective.

So the citizen sued the policeman civilly for twenty-five thousand dollars on the ground that the patrolman "deliberately and recklessly" issued a summons to him when, under the circumstances as they existed, he didn't deserve one, and thereby caused the plaintiff to suffer "great emotional anguish."

This left the *policeman* with a problem: Is it better to pay a possible verdict or be a rotten egg?

A GRAPHIC DEFENSE

A RECENT, AIRTIGHT defense to a drunken driving charge was all the more startling because the case against the man was airtight too.

It certainly seemed impossible to beat this case, for

37

when the man was brought in they wheeled out the Police Drunkometer and his breath zoomed the needle up to a reading of .246, which is higher than a kite, as you are officially drunk at .150.

But this defendant, who weighed 238 pounds, claimed a man of his weight can take much more whisky than a standard-sized citizen.

On the witness stand he opened a brief case and laid out three pints of 86-proof whisky and a shot glass. Ice water for chasers was provided by the court.

This man began drinking his testimony, glass by glass, until he reached the respectable total of twenty. Then the judge called for a reading at the Drunkometer.

The reading: .122 — not drunk.

Well, this particular defendant certainly proved that either the Drunkometer, which read .246 when he was arrested, was out of order and not a valid test, or that the vision of the policeman who read the meter was not twenty-twenty, since it was obvious that there wasn't enough whisky around to make this citizen touch .246.

It also shows the fallacy of applying an open-and-shut, you-did-or-you-didn't rule of law to all defendants.

Suppose this remarkable defendant visits a friend who is nearly fresh out of whisky, and takes *one* lonely shot, then gets into his car and drives away. On the road he has an accident. Someone detects liquor on his breath, and he is charged with drunken driving. He cannot deny the liquor on his breath, but to say that this man was guilty of the charge would certainly be, as we have seen, pre-posterous.

Yet another citizen, with that same lonely shot, could be definitely drunk, or drunk enough to be charged with drunken driving.

There are all kinds of people.

38

SAD CASE OF THE SMILING LAWYER

AN EVEN more remarkable witness for the defense illustrates that smiling too soon is sometimes premature.

This witness was being cross-examined, and was testifying with supreme confidence and aplomb, and his answers stretched credulity to the breaking point:

Q: Let us go over your testimony of this morning, sir. You know that the serial number of the bond was CR47612973 *because you caught a glimpse of it sticking out of this man's pocket!*

A: CR47614973.

Q: Thank you. You never wrote it down anywhere?

A: No, sir.

Q: But you recall it precisely!

A: Precisely.

Q: You have given us the names — the full names — of everyone in the room at the time, all *seven!*

A: Yes, sir.

Q: Though you met them just that once?

A: That once.

Q: And last but not least, the license number of the automobile, which you saw at an angle, in the dark, as it sped around the corner!

A: That is correct.

Q: The number being DY93758 NY?

A: DY937568 NY.

Q: You never wrote any of these things down?

A: No, sir.

Q: Remembered everything!

A: Everything.

At this point the lawyer had it solved: the witness was an idiot and simply didn't realize how silly these answers were. So the lawyer smiled faintly, glanced significantly at the jury, paused briefly for the right effect and asked his next question: "Tell me, sir, you're not a memory expert by any chance, are you?" The answer is probably still ringing in the poor man's ears:

A: Yes, sir.

Q: *What!*

A: My stage name is Memoire. Would you like a demonstration? You have thirteen stripes in your tie, your left shoe lace is untied, the judge is wearing a blue shirt under his robe, we adjourned yesterday at 4:37 P.M. and began this morning at 10:03 A.M. Have you a dollar bill in your pocket? Ah, thank you. Now I will glance at the serial number for a half-second. There. Now I will tell you the number — backwards: J 45223578 E. Is it correct, sir? Thank you. Now, if you have two other bills, kindly hold them up together so that the number will be twice as long —

In a few short months this lawyer was himself again, and he is still in practice. But he *never* smiles.

WATCH YOUR LANGUAGE

AROUND A courtroom, *insurance* is practically a dirty word, because the jurors are not supposed to know there is insurance in a case, lest they give away money like drunken soldiers (*see* Statistics on Military Personnel, Revised).

So that when you are sued, the insurance company, who is defending you, has a right to keep secret from the jury the fact that you are insured. (In rare cases they waive that right and disclose the fact, but the insurance company is the only one who can do this. If anyone else does it during the trial, it will result in a mistrial.)

This is why you may walk into a courtroom one day to get out of the rain and hear this:

Q: Are you on friendly terms with your mother, Mr. Flabgast?
A: Why, of course.
Q: Never quarreled?
A: Of course not.
Q: You visit —
A: Regularly.
Q: Everything fine?
A: Why, of course.
Q: But you are suing her for fifty thousand dollars because she dropped the piano on your finger while you were adjusting the casters?
A: Well, if she didn't let go so soon —
Q: You want fifty thousand dollars from your mother!
A: Well, the pain —

41

Because of this legal bar to disclosing the fact of insurance, the poor lawyer for the plaintiff is in an awful spot on summation. What he would *like* to say to the jury is this:

Ladies and gentlemen: What kind of a monster do they want you to believe this man is! Does my client look like the kind of a man who would take his mother's last dime and leave her to starve in her old age? Really! He wants the *insurance company* to pay him for this finger. That's what the policy is for! Did you ever try to play a saxaphone with a finger —

That's what he would *like* to say. But he must stand up there and say this:

Ladies and gentlemen: I know it looks pretty bad, having to sue your own mother for fifty thousand dollars, but after all, this is not a place for sentiment. Justice is blind, you know. And another thing, she had no right to drop this piano — right on his finger — her own son — she knew he was there. And furthermore —

The lawyer not only looks foolish, he feels foolish. But rules are rules.

Sometimes the rule doesn't work out too well for the insurance company because back in the jury room a lively discussion is going on:

JUROR NO. 3: I say give him the fifty thousand — and all expenses.

JUROR NO. 4: Just like that, eh? And what about his mother? Did you see that little old lady? Why she could hardly —

JUROR NO. 3: Really, mister, you must be from out of town or something! You ever hear of insurance? Didn't that tall character look like an insurance lawyer to you? Didn't you get that suit, and those glasses with the ribbon? Did you notice his brief case? And what kind of a man would sue his own mother?

JUROR NO. 4: It's been done.

JUROR NO. 8: That's a fact. I read of a case —

JUROR NO. 3: I don't care what you read. I'm talking about this case.

JUROR NO. 4: It's been done. There are people will sue anybody.

JUROR NO. 3: But this old lady is a charwoman! Where is she going to get fifty thousand dollars?

JUROR NO. 9: That's not up to us. We'll have enough trouble deciding this case. You're forgetting the judge's charge, my friend. A case must be decided strictly on the evidence. There has been absolutely no evidence here about insurance. Now, strictly on the evidence, I didn't like this man's case. Why was his *mother* lifting the piano anyway? Why didn't *he* —

JUROR NO. 11: Say, I never thought of that —

JUROR NO. 3: Let's get back to the policy. Every policy —

JUROR NO. 9: What on earth are you talking about?

JUROR NO. 3: You know damn well what I'm talking about, mister. Insurance. There's plenty of insurance here and I say make 'em pay . . .

The company always hopes that this sort of thing won't take place in the jury room, so the fact of insurance is not mentioned. But this strategy is a calculated risk. Later on we shall see what takes place when the fact is deliberately disclosed by the company and why they do it.

3

WHEN YOU ARE THE PLAINTIFF

THE BIG thing about being the plaintiff is that you have the burden of proof; that is, you must prove it happened the way you say because you are the one who is suing. If, for example, you say that Snodgrass was in the room at the time and he says he was not, you must prove that he was. You might bring another witness to say so, or you might show his footprints in the dust or his handwriting on the wall or you might be a stunning blonde, but you have the burden of proving what you allege.

And before you can collect any money, there are a number of particular things that must be proven and the lack of one single item may ruin your whole case, so it might be well to look into this matter with some care.

There are a good many strange notions on this subject.

45

Joe Lethercote, accompanied by six companions, enters the Perfect Food Cafeteria. They make their choices and bring the food to a large, round table. Let us keep our eye on Joe.

He has selected an elaborate ring of Danish pastry. He is about to halve it with knife and fork. Suddenly he puts down the knife and fork, his lips compressed, his eyes ablaze. With thumb and forefinger he gingerly extracts from the Danish pastry a long, rusty tenpenny nail and holds it aloft for all to see.

Now the sound track:

JOE: How do you like that!

FRANK: A nail!

MARTY: A rusty nail!

SAM: What do you expect in a dump?

JOE: I coulda swallowed it!

BERT: You coulda broke a toot!

JOE: They ain't gonna get away with this! What do they think this is?

FRANK: You can get plenty.

MARTY: He *should* get plenty. How would *you* like to swallow a nail?

TOM: He didn't swallow no nail.

FRANK: What do you mean he didn't swallow no nail? He coulda. And what about if he cut up his gums and his mouth? You mean if a dump hands out this kind of food you gotta eat it?

TOM: Who said you have to eat anything? Nobody has et anything. What is all the shooting for?

JOE: You talk like a Communist, you know that? I coulda been stabbed in the throat.

MARTY: Well, wait a minute. Are you hurt in any manner? Are you damaged by anything?

46

JOE: How do you like this! What am I surrounded by? Is this a public restaurant, or what is it? Are you trying to say that I have to eat a Danish pastry with a nail in it?

MARTY: Well, don't eat it.

JOE: I see. Funny.

FRANK: Joe is right. What is the Board of Health for? A customer is entitled to sanitary food — no two ways about it. Why, if he walks into court with that rusty nail and says it was in the Danish pastry, what do *you* think? With six witnesses too. Don't forget *that*.

The animated discussion breaks up at three o'clock in the morning, by which time Joe is convinced that the Perfect Food Cafeteria, Inc. should be compelled to explain the whole thing to a court and jury. So he wraps the rusty nail carefully in a paper napkin and goes home.

At ten o'clock in the morning Joe is in a lawyer's office, rusty nail, witnesses and all. And ten minutes later he is walking down the street, a sadly disillusioned man, for the lawyer has refused to take his case.

It was a perfect case, too, except for one little thing: there was no damage. The cafeteria certainly had no right to serve the rusty nail, but nothing whatever has *happened* to Joe by reason of it and so no one owes him a nickel.

A five-ton safe may fall from a thirty-story building and just miss your skull by a hair's breadth. You'd be scared and incoherent and fighting mad, but you couldn't collect a cent. No damage.

Looking a bit closer into the possibilities of Joe's discovery, suppose Joe had actually bit into the pastry and discovered the nail in that way.

He now has a perfect case. But just a moment. Is it worth bothering with? His gum is bleeding, to be sure, and it hurts a little, and he is greatly annoyed.

But what could he get for an injury like that? The gum heals in a few hours or a day or two. He has been slightly inconvenienced; he practically forgets the incident in a day or two. What could a jury possibly give him? What would *you* give him? If a jury gave him more than twenty-five or fifty dollars it would surprise everyone in the courtroom — except Joe. Joe would be up to his ears in four figures right up to the moment of the verdict.

Assume he got a hundred dollars. There is the lawyer's fee, which might run as high as half of the money received on such a small claim as this. Joe has lost a day from his work; his witnesses have had to make the same sacrifice — and there may have been postponements (there always are a few). There was carfare to and from court, lunch money for several people, and Joe has had to wait several months or a year for a trial.

On top of all this, the case may be appealed, since the restaurant may decide to appeal on principle — and that will mean another wait of six months or more. After all of which it might be that the cafeteria has been running at a loss for some time and is so broke it can't pay the judgment.

There's more.

Suppose Joe had broken a tooth? The verdict might be just enough to allow him to replace it. But how about the dentist's fee for coming to court? You couldn't expect to drag a dentist to court to talk about Joe's tooth for nothing.

If two teeth are broken, Joe begins to move over into the black, for the dentist's fee can be amortized over the slightly larger verdict.

If three teeth are broken, Joe really has a lawsuit, but he'd have an even better one with a broken leg, if you want to push this thing far enough.

48

JACKPOT

IT IS ASTONISHING how a man's values change when he becomes a plaintiff. A party who has never actually touched a fifty-dollar bill with his bare hands suddenly finds himself suing for damages and cannot remember if money comes in denominations smaller than one thousand dollars.

Often the reason for this phenomenon is the fact that a friend, at one time or another, has received a large verdict in a lawsuit for seemingly similar injuries (which later turn out to be quite different). Sometimes a newspaper article, carelessly written, will tell of a very large verdict for personal injuries. Many people read it and are impressed by the amount. A recent news item read this way:

Miss Harriet Finley of 2321 Choctaw Drive was awarded seventy-eight thousand dollars for personal injuries resulting from her fall in the Crown Department Store on December 16th last, in which it was alleged she sustained serious injuries, including a broken arm which interfered with her work as a model. This is believed to be one of the largest verdicts of its kind in this area. Attorneys for the store announced the verdict will be appealed.

It is possible the make-up man at this newspaper couldn't spare more space for this particular item. He might have said to the reporter, "I am cutting your pratt-fall story down to seventy-five words; need the space."

And it is a safe bet that thousands of citizens came away with distorted ideas about money. The reporter's

49

original story might have shown two broken legs with compound fractures, and so badly broken the woman will go through life bent over; a severe skull fracture, nearly severing the head, and most uncomfortable, and a paralysis of the entire right arm.

Seventy-eight thousand is a lot of money even in counterfeit bills, and a party must be hurt seriously to get it, and many will say she is welcome to it.

People read such items too quickly, or jump to improper conclusions. Because Uncle Henry got twelve hundred dollars for falling down those stairs in the dark doesn't mean that Aunt Kate will get the same amount for that slide for life on the wet turnip in the supermarket. A couple of dozen assorted factors may change the complexion of things. Yet how often we hear this:

"What do you mean I may get nothing! What about Charley? Didn't he have exactly the same case? Didn't he slip on a banana peel too? Why, he even fell the same way I did. It's uncanny. I'll get the same lawyer is what I'll do."

Actually this lady will have rough going. She was descending the stairway of an apartment house. Suddenly, at the third step, she slipped on a banana peel and broke her neck. In three places.

She has no case, unless she can prove that the banana peel was on that step long enough for the landlord to know about it and that he failed to have it removed within a reasonable time. To be perfectly preposterous about it: Suppose she opens her door to leave her apartment, sees a banana peel, retraces her steps, calls the landlord or superintendent on the phone and demands that he remove it. He races upstairs without delay and removes it.

While she is powdering her nose for a second exit, a neighbor who is wild about bananas, throws out another

50

skin. Our unfortunate subject slides on this skin. Who is going to say the landlord is negligent? He knew nothing about it. Nobody told him, and it wasn't there long enough for him to find out.

MORE NOTIONS

MANY PEOPLE think that if they send somebody a telegram and it is not delivered, or delivered late, they have hit the jackpot and do not have to work any more.

This is not so.

You can only be paid for the actual damage the non-delivery has caused, even if you win.

If you send your Aunt Kate a telegram urging her to come to a shotgun wedding and she doesn't get it, she may not come, but you cannot say: "Now Aunt Kate doesn't speak to me any more and I value her friendship at $325,000."

It would be silly, because anybody whose friendship is worth that much must be pretty smart and would understand about a non-delivered telegram and forgive you.

Suppose the telegram were delivered, but not promptly, and Aunt Kate, realizing she will be late if she doesn't hurry, flies to the wedding on the next plane. The plane crashes and she is badly hurt.

There is no claim against the telegraph company; they didn't tell her to fly. They didn't even recommend she go to the wedding.

The pity of it is that a shotgun wedding is not even legal or binding and the whole thing was for nothing in the first place.

If you send a telegram to Uncle John demanding that he sell the uranium stocks at once at the current market price and it is delivered too late for him to do so, and he is compelled to sell at a lower price, you may recover the difference between the two prices, provided you can prove gross negligence against the telegraph company — that their conduct was willfully, unreasonably careless and negligent — and how on earth are you going to do that?

TO EACH HIS OWN

THE THING that is so little understood is this: Each individual case stands on its own feet, and there can be no blanket declaration of law that will fit every case. There are of course general statements of the law covering certain *types* of cases, but all of the elements required by the law must fall into place, all of the items required by the law must be proved before there can be a recovery.

This is a very important proposition, for it is the one great mistake the layman makes in considering a lawsuit. Nine factors in your lawsuit may be exactly the same as the one that gave the other man $100,000, but the last little factor may make it different and lose it for you.

Lawyers spend hours, days and months digging the law out of vast libraries, seeking to find a case "on all fours" as they say; legal specialists work laboriously over erudite briefs and trial memoranda to submit to the learned court; opposing counsel labor in research; the court reads these documents and listens to scholarly argument concerning them; then the judge himself explores his own library to make sure before rendering a decision — which may be either affirmed or reversed by a higher court.

But the layman will stand on the corner of Fourth and Main, near Sam's cigar store, and promptly render an opinion on any case under the sun: "This case? Can't lose.

Same as Tom's in Chicago. Tom won that one. Common sense; a company has no right to do a thing like that."

ANOTHER MISTAKE

SPEAKING OF mistakes, here is one that is made in many cases and helps to lose them: too many angles.

If a story has too many ramifications it is hard to follow. What is worse, it may create the idea that the teller of the story wants to make sure of winning and is throwing in everything.

A lady is suing her landlord because she fell on a broken step. That is a simple story, and there are just a few simple items involved in it:

Was the step broken?

Did the landlord know it was broken?

Did the lady fall?

Was she injured?

If the lady stuck to those four points and hammered away at them, she might get somewhere with the jury. But what does she do? How does she keep the attention of the jurors focused on those four simple points?

Like this:

Q: Now, madam, was the step broken?

A: Broken! Let me tell you, everybody in the house knew that if you —

Q: The step, madam; was it broken?

A: Not only was the step broken, but everything about that rotten building was in bad shape. Do you know how those halls looked? Why, my sister and I —

Q: Did you fall on the step, madam?

53

A: Now, *there's* a question! What would I be doing here? Did I fall! Every time —

Q: Did you?

A: Did I what?

Q: Did you fall?

A: Of course I fell. And when I told him about it he insulted me. He insults everybody. He told one tenant, in my presence —

Q: Were you hurt, madam?

A: I haven't been the same since.

Q: Where were you hurt?

A: Well! My knees were bruised, awfully bruised. They still bother me in rainy weather. My arms were scraped, both arms; you can see the scar up here — no, that is the vaccination — up here — well, there *was* a scar. I'm so nervous; I've never been in court, you know. My forehead was cut and bleeding. Why, a neighbor saw that blood and would you like to know what she said?

Q: Thank you, no. Where else?

A: My back, too; I can't lie comfortably on it to this day. I get these shooting pains all the time. The last time —

Q: Had you told the landlord about that broken step?

A: A thousand times, and my husband told him, too, and every tenant in the house has been insulted by that man —

Now, this lady is not helping the jury, her lawyer or herself. She has made that whole house a shambles; she has made the landlord an ogre; she has spilled blood all over the place; she has dragged in the neighbors — all of them; she has given the landlord one thousand warnings — which at the rate of a warning a day would take more than three years; and she has never been in court before.

The jury must now begin discounting and subtracting from her story, and they might well subtract her out of court.

It is not merely a question of exaggeration — *that* is so bad it belongs by itself; it is a question of bringing in matters which have nothing to do with the case. The lady cannot collect for the insults. She cannot collect for the condition of the halls. She cannot collect for the insults to the neighbors. She cannot collect for the roof, or the lobby. Her action revolves around that *step*.

The same thing goes for the landlord in this case. He might say the lady never pays her rent on time, that she is an insufferable scold, that her television set has never been turned off or turned down since she moved in, that *she* insults *him,* that the entire building is kept as new and shiny as a fire engine and that no steps are *ever* broken.

If he does that, the jury may subtract from him and add on to the lady, and she may get twenty-five dollars.

So the big idea is to stay on the main highway, which is the story of your accident, and not go traipsing off into side roads that lead to nowhere. Pretend you are a train — an express train: First Stop, the Accident; Second Stop, the Pain and Suffering; Third Stop, the Verdict; Last Stop, the Bank.

ANOTHER NOTION

MANY PEOPLE think that an affidavit or a doctor's certificate is good in a trial. They are not. The testimony must be produced — live.

And for a very good reason: Opposing counsel has the right to cross-examine your witnesses. John Roomur might make an affidavit that a certain party is a skunk, beats his mother and has been on the bum for eighteen years. Roomur might swear to these items before a notary public. You cannot wave that affidavit before a jury in a courtroom, because if Roomur himself were produced, he might testify as follows:

Q: Is John Roomur your real name?
A: Who, me?
Q: You don't hear well, do you?
A: Sure I do.
Q: Answer the question, then.
A: Well, it used to be Henry Plunk, but that don't —
Q: Do you work?
A: In a way.
Q: What way?
A: Do I have to tell?
Q: I think so.
A: Well, I shoot pool.
Q: Indeed! A gambler!
A: No gambler. The way I play is not gambling.

Q: Please explain.

A: I hustle the game. I bet a few quarters and lose; then I bet a few dollars and win. That is not gambling.

Q: How old are you, please?

A: Twenty-seven.

Q: How long have you been engaged in your — your profession?

A: About eighteen years.

Q: You started at nine!

A: Well, it ain't my fault if I was cooped up in a school all them years.

Q: By the way, do *you* beat your mother?

A: I ain't laid a hand on her in a year. I can prove it, because I ain't been home in a year.

The jury would read Roomur's affidavit with a bit more care after that cross-examination.

The doctor's certificate is slightly different, but the principle is the same. The doctor might certify that the plaintiff had tuberculosis and fallen arches, and the cross-examination might bring out the fact that the doctor has

57

been in practice only three days. The plaintiff might indeed have tuberculosis and fallen arches, but the jury would have a right to weigh that young doctor's testimony against the testimony of the doctor for the other side, who boasts of forty years' experience and says it wasn't tuberculosis and fallen arches, but a whisky wheeze and bar-fly bends.

WHAT IS AN INJURY WORTH?

THERE IS A difference of opinion on this matter. We can see this by looking in on a few random summations:

Members of the jury: My client is asking you to award him three thousand dollars for a fractured wrist. He says he suffered excruciating pain and was caused the most upsetting inconvenience by this injury; that the wrist will never again be the same flexible, useful member that it was; that he has suffered and will continue to suffer a severe loss in earning power by reason of this painful, disabling injury.

58

Remember, ladies and gentlemen, that my client is a trombone player, and a good one, or was before this accident. It is the only profession he knows. He toiled and labored for years to attain the perfection that was his before this speeder ran him down, and now he must suffer with this injury to the end of his days — and nights — and his music must suffer, too.

What would *you* take for a fractured wrist, ladies and gentlemen? If I placed three one-thousand-dollar bills and a sledge hammer upon this jury box and suggested that you could pick up those bills if you would stand for a blow on your right wrist with that sledge hammer, tell me truthfully, would you do it?

A *fracture*, now; not just a blow. You take it on the wrist until we produce a fracture, a compound fracture, to be specific; and a contusion or abrasion or laceration or linear fracture doesn't count; you must take a compound fracture before you can take those bills!

Tell me, sir, would *you* do that? Would *you, sir?* Madam, would *you?* Or *you? Any* of you?

Of course not! What kind of people would you be!

Pay this man, ladies and gentlemen; pay him, as you would want to be paid for a compound fracture of the right wrist. I thank you.

Pretty good, what? But here is the summation of the other lawyer in the same case:

Members of the jury: This man wants you to give him three thousand dollars for a broken wrist! *Three thousand dollars!*

I have tried many cases, ladies and gentlemen, possibly not as many as my experienced friend, but many.

59

Never in my courtroom life have I seen such unmitigated gall! *Three thousand dollars!*

Let us see what he wants all this money for. He had a broken wrist — a *fractured* wrist; let's make it sound as serious as possible. Notice that I say he "had" one. His own doctor admitted on cross-examination that sometimes a fractured bone may heal together in such a way that the callus formation will make the whole thing stronger than it was before! *Three thousand dollars!*

He played a trombone in a third-rate band all his adult life and earned less than a second-rate handyman. Perfection is it! Music indeed!

As for the excruciating pain and suffering. Well, let me tell you, in all the cases I have tried, it is a strange coincidence, but I have yet to hear them mention any other kind of pain. It is always excruciating. It is never *considerable* pain, or *severe* pain, or even *awful* pain. It is *excruciating* pain. These plaintiffs will settle for nothing less. They must have excruciating pain or none at all. I tell you, I'm beginning to feel a touch of it myself.

What kind of pain do you suppose this trombone player had when at the age of nine he blocked a few uppercuts with his face? What kind of pain was it when he was pushed from the swing and fell to the concrete walk? What did he call it when he caught that brick at the back of his head? He didn't ask for three thousand dollars *then,* did he?

And how many similar items do you suppose he left out of his testimony?

As to my friend's dramatic offer to break your wrist with a sledge hammer, ladies and gentlemen, *really!*

Certainly you wouldn't cold-bloodedly let him crack your

wrist with a sledge hammer! If such a thing had been done to this plaintiff, I myself would recommend a few dollars.

But this plaintiff didn't receive his injury that way. He got it before he knew it, and it was set by the doctors before he knew it, and nature's wonderful healing process was under way before he knew it.

Three thousand dollars! I would not believe it if I had not heard it with my own ears! I hope he has a better idea about music than he has about the value of money.

Throw this trombone player out of court, ladies and gentlemen, because he was drunk at the time of the accident anyway, as our witnesses testified.

I thank you.

These jurors will not be home early, and some of them may need alibis, which are covered in the chapter on Marriage Is What You Make It.

Another set:

Ladies and gentlemen: This young girl is seeking an award at your hands for three stitches in her scalp, plus the excruciating pain and suffering that you have heard described.

Let us for the moment lay aside the torturous agony that must have been hers as a result of these wounds and see what else they mean to this young, attractive girl. She is unmarried. This is very important, ladies and gentlemen. It is the birthright of every girl to have a husband, and it is a right which is not always realized. It is difficult, and a girl needs every ounce of charm and beauty to accomplish this worthy goal. This young girl's chances are hurt, ladies and gentlemen; they are hurt as she herself was hurt by this wound in her scalp.

61

The mighty power that arranges these things may find her a husband, but this careless defendant, this callous motorist, has placed an obstacle in her path. We must not forget that.

What are you going to give her for these stitches? It is easy to say "stitches," just a small word. But what are they actually? First there is the awful impact itself, the tearing, ripping of the skin from the scalp, just under which lie the delicate brain cells which must not be disturbed, lest havoc and chaos result.

Then comes the indescribable agony of suffering and pain; then, as if that were not enough, comes the doctor with his long, sharp needle and thread to calmly insert it into the already wounded flesh and sew it together. Then the pain, and the waiting and worrying while it slowly tries to mend. And finally the awful scar, the permanent scar on this young, unmarried girl's scalp.

That is what stitches are, ladies and gentlemen. That is what this unmarried girl wants to be compensated for. What are you going to give her? I will not suggest how many thousands. That is up to you. I say in all sincerity: Let your conscience be your guide.

I thank you.

Don't go. Two sides to every case. Also two summations:

Ladies and gentlemen: This lady has three stitches in her head. Nobody denies that. She showed them to us, though that was a difficult job. They are concealed so neatly beneath her rich, luxuriant black hair that it took her eleven minutes to find them. I timed it. Eleven minutes! Look at your watch, sir, when you go up to the jury room and see how long eleven minutes are.

And don't be carried away by that bizarre description of the stitches by my imaginative friend. It doesn't mean anything.

In the first place, there wasn't any awful impact. The door handle just grazed her skin and parted it a bit, so that suturing was the thing to do about it. And the delicate brain cells are protected by a bone as thick as the stack of bills that she wants for this trivial case. Thirdly, the doctor didn't creep up on her with a hunting knife; the whole transaction took half a minute and probably didn't involve much more than the removal of a splinter from your thumb.

And there was no waiting or worrying while it slowly tried to mend, because this lady was out dancing two nights later with that well-dressed young man who denied under oath that he was her fiancé, and whom I will not characterize further.

This *young girl* is not as young as my tearful friend would have you believe, either. He forgot she said she was twenty-eight. And she was twenty-eight before we touched her. Does he want us to find her a husband? Does he want us to give her an annuity?

Give her something if you must, but, ladies and gentlemen, I say fifty dollars a stitch would more than do it.

Yes, there is a difference of opinion.

THE DEATH CASE

A STRIKING illustration of the value of an injury is afforded in the ordinary death case. A man may be struck by an automobile and die. He may have been the nicest man in the world, a faithful husband and the devoted father of four children. The whole neighborhood may have thought highly of this man. Yet these things are not the measure of the value of his life.

His widow will bring an action to recover for the loss of this fine man, and at the trial the following matters will be considered:

How old was he at the time of death?

How much longer could he expect to live?

What had been his earning capacity up to that time?

How much money would he have earned had he remained alive and continued working?

So that if the poor man, splendid though he was, happened to have been a porter, earning thirty-five dollars a week most of his life, the likelihood is that he would have continued to earn that sum had he lived.

Now, if his death occurred at the age of forty-seven, experts would swear that he could have expected to live approximately twenty-three years more. Assuming that he continued to be employed those twenty-three years, with no layoffs for illness, strikes or other reasons, he would have earned in those twenty-three years the sum of $41,860.

That is about the sum the widow would be entitled to, unless the jury decided to deduct a few thousand on the theory of possible non-employment here and there in the twenty-three years. She might receive twenty-five thousand, or thirty. Certainly not nearly the amount she had in mind for her irreparable loss.

She cannot be paid for the grief and the subsequent loneliness and widowhood; she can be compensated only for the loss of her husband's earnings.

Now, suppose this man were a banker, with an income of fifty thousand dollars a year, and suppose he had been

the meanest man in the world, that he took pleasure in foreclosing mortgages, shoplifting in the five-and-ten, taking candy from babies and stealing pennies from blind men. If he died at the age of forty-seven the same method of valuation would be used — up to a certain point. That is to say, for twenty-three years his earnings would come to $1,150,000, which is a lot of money even when you say it fast; and there is an approximate maximum in such cases when the figures get that big.

So that the widow of the banker would probably recover enough money to enable her to live out her life in the style to which she had been accustomed by her banker-husband's magnificent income.

All of which is probably fair enough, because the broad theory of the law is that the jury must try to make you whole again — that is, restore you to the way you were before the happening.

Naturally, this is often not possible, in the strictest sense — for example, if your arm is broken they cannot give you a new arm; so they do the next best thing: pay you for your pain and suffering, medical expenses, loss of time, and so on.

And if you are bereaved, they cannot restore the loved one, but they can restore the material benefits of which you have been deprived.

THE GUEST CASE

THE GUEST CASE is a difficult case to win. In the guest case you give somebody a ride in your car and he bumps his head on getting out and sues you for damages.

Or you invite the boss over for dinner on a very cold evening, and your clumsy maid, thinking to warm him up fast, serves the hot soup down his collar and he resents it.

It is a hard case to win because who likes a man who will sue his host after a kindness or a bit of hospitality?

Yet, under the law, a guest is entitled to as much relief and protection as anyone else, because a guest is a person, and all persons are equal in the eyes of the law.

But it is still a hard case to win. Let us look at the testimony of a witness in a guest case and see if we like it.

Q: Now sir, just sit back in your chair. You say that as the car in which you were riding approached Route 66 it skidded into a ditch and you were injured?
A: Yes, sir.
Q: Who drove the car?
A: Mr. Maximus.
Q: Your brother.
A: Well, yes, sir.
Q: And you claim the speed of the car was so great that when he attempted to apply the brakes, the car skidded and went into the ditch?

66

A: Yes, sir.

Q: How fast was your brother driving?

A: Seventy-five miles an hour.

Q: Did you say anything to him at any time about this terrific speed?

A: Certainly. I told him to cut it out. I told him he would kill us both. I told him to stop the car and let me out. He just laughed.

Q: And you want your brother to pay you ten thousand dollars for your injuries!

A: Well, if a man —

Q: The question was: You want your brother to pay you ten thousand dollars!

A: Well, yes.

Q: Are you on friendly terms with your brother now?

A: Well —

Q: Please answer.

A: Well, yes; I have nothing against him.

Q: You asked him to stop driving so fast; you begged him to let you out of the car, and he just laughed, and you were hurt, and you want ten thousand dollars from him — but you have nothing against him!

A: Well, anybody —

Q: The question, please.

A: Well, that's right.

Q: You like him!

A: He is my brother. A brother is a brother.

Q: And ten thousand is ten thousand, eh?

A: Well —

This case is difficult because the brother, who owns the car, is insured. But the jury, as we have seen, is not permitted to know that. In the eyes of the law, a litigant is a litigant, whether he is insured or not. It must not be divulged to the jury that there is insurance in the case.

In this particular case, the defendant's lawyer (who really represents the insurance company) has decided to divulge it and risk everything on a particular theory he wants to leave with the jury:

Members of the jury: Don't you see what goes on here? These bright lads, these amiable brothers, are bowling along in this patched-up convertible and begin to think about how nice it would be to have a new one, a Jaguar maybe. Suddenly the car swerves or something, and they do or don't find themselves in the roadway. Then Bert gets a brilliant idea: "The insurance company! Millions! We'll sue! Or, more specifically, *I'll* sue *you*." And here we are.

But they make a mistake! They reckon without the intelligence and character of the American juror!

Show them —

But the other lawyer has a few words to say. His hair is white; his voice is rich and throaty; he stands up straight and true; he has been doing this for a long time:

Ladies and gentlemen: I am relieved that my eloquent friend has finally concluded his remarks. I have been confused. For a while there he had me believing I was in a criminal case, representing a couple of holdup men; the James brothers maybe, or the Dalton boys, complete with six-shooters and masks.

But what have we here? We have two brothers, family men, taxpayers, American citizens.

Now, I represent only one of these brothers, the one who was injured. I have nothing whatever to do with the other fellow, this Kurt.

68

Yet Kurt interests me more than my own client. I can't get him out of my thoughts. His position here fascinates me.

You see, Kurt here is something more than a taxpayer. He is also a *premium* payer!

Now, throughout this trial I have been fascinated by one little thing about this *premium* payer, as he sits here at the table. I haven't been able to take my eyes off it — and I wonder whether you too have been struck by it. It is such a trifling, commonplace thing — but it has enormous significance here: I refer to the hole in his left shoe!

As I sat here for three days gazing at that hole in the shoe of this *premium* payer, a picture appeared before my mind's eye: I saw this family man, with a wife and all those children, feeling the bitter cold of the wet snow through the hole in that shoe! I saw him standing before a shoe store and deciding he could endure it no longer. I saw him consult his budget carefully, hesitate at the threshold of the store, and resolutely turn away.

In my imagining, I heard him talk to his wife when he came home:

"Don't tell me you're still wearing those torn shoes!"

"I'm afraid so, dear."

"Why, in heaven's name?"

"Well, Martha, this is premium week, that's why! If I should hurt someone while driving, how would we feel if we couldn't pay! I *must* keep up the insurance! I'll do without shoes, but I'll keep those premiums going!"

Ladies and gentlemen, those are the thoughts that came to me as I saw that hole in the shoe!

THE COURT: Oh, brother!

COUNSEL: I beg Your Honor's pardon?

THE COURT: Just clearing my throat, sir. Carry on.

COUNSEL: Thank you . . . yes . . . well, we have no quarrel with a man paying his bills, and a premium is a bill to be paid, and there is no particular nobility attached to it, and the insurance company is entitled to have it — because, after all, they are going to pay anyone who is hurt by their *premium* payer!

Ah, but no! Not *any*one! Anyone but his *own brother!* He can *kill* his own brother with this rolling junk-heap, he can *maim* him — the brother who saved his life during the war, the brother who donated his blood —

THE COURT: Really, Counselor —

COUNSEL: Well, perhaps so, Judge. . . . Anyway, members of the jury, they want to exclude this man's brother from the benefits of this policy! From the fruits of these never-failing *premiums!* They signed a legal contract with this man: You keep paying us premiums, we'll take care of your accidents.

Now they want to weasel out of it — they want to welch on the deal — they want to renege; they used to be proud to call this *premium* payer one of *their* premium payers — now they disown him! They turn him out into the cold —

THE COURT: Counselor, don't you think —

COUNSEL: You have a point there, Judge. . . . Well, ladies and gentlemen, show this insurance company that a contract is a sacred document in the good old U.S.A., that our Constitution lives on! That our proud flag —

THE COURT: Counselor, the luncheon hour is about —

COUNSEL: Splendid, Judge, splendid! I am quite agreeable to suspending at this time. I shall not require more than a couple of hours when we resume again —

Oh, there will be plenty of excitement in the jury room.

A RUNNING START

WHATEVER YOU are suing about, the important part of your case will be the beginning. To paraphrase the Book — *As ye start so shall ye finish.*

In an ordinary negligence case, after the plaintiff has

given his name and address and answered a few preliminary questions, he will be asked the following question:

Q: Now tell us briefly what happened.

Around the answer to that question will revolve the whole case. More cases have been lost on that one answer than you could count. This is why:

To bring a lawsuit a plaintiff must draw up a complaint, in which he must allege fairly definitely what happened to him.

Now, if in the complaint he says he *tripped,* he must *trip* on the witness stand. Not literally, of course, but his story on the stand must coincide with that in his complaint. He cannot say he *slipped* or did something else.

Here is a flash of what might happen if the wrong answer were made to this all-important question:

Q: Now tell us briefly, in your own words, just what happened.

A: Well, there was this toe-trap, and before I knew it I slipped and went sprawling on my face —

A pretty short answer, but the plaintiff has done it! He has spoiled his case, because when he is through testifying, the defendant's lawyer will say:

"If Your Honor please, I move to strike out this witness's entire testimony, on the ground that it does not conform to the allegations in his complaint."

Now follows a long, legal argument addressed to this proposition, and the court, desiring to see substantial justice done, will allow the plaintiff's lawyer to conform the pleadings to the proof, which means that the complaint is now technically changed to *slipping.*

But, though the plaintiff has corrected his technical position and has saved his case from being thrown out of court, he has not done a thing for his practical position, for here is the defendant's lawyer's summation:

Members of the jury: This man has convicted himself out of his own mouth. He has given himself away. I didn't trip him. And the *City* didn't trip him. He tripped himself. And he didn't do it on that sidewalk, either. He did it when he said he *slipped!* And this was not just a slip of the tongue. You will recall the testimony. It was a wet day; it was raining. We have been contending that we didn't know how this accident happened, except that it didn't happen as this man alleges in his complaint. Now we *know!* He *slipped.* He said so himself!

If he had tripped by reason of this toe-trap, he would have said, "I tripped." But he says, "I slipped." Throw him out.

And they might.

So it is important to answer that first question carefully. The words, once uttered, cannot be recalled. Of course your lawyer will go over this with you before the trial, when he checks all the papers and gets the case ready, but it is a question of remembering these things and getting them right.

FROM THE FILES

SPEAKING OF toe-traps and tripping, right out of the files comes a reminder that sometimes a trivial thing may upset the most beautiful lawsuit. It may not lose the case, but it may put an awful crimp in it.

This man was suing a municipality for several thousand dollars. He claimed the city had allowed a dangerous toe-trap to exist on a busy street; that he was a victim of this dangerous toe-trap and had sustained severe injuries, to say nothing of pain and suffering.

The case went in nicely. The city's lawyer went to work on cross-examination:

Q: A toe-trap, eh?

A: That's right.

Q: Describe it.

A: Well, it was a break in the sidewalk; one of the flagstones was broken and sunken in, and the other part stuck up a couple of inches at least. I went sprawling before I knew what happened.

Q: Then you examined this toe-trap?

A: Sure.

Q: Stuck up two inches?

A: At least.

Q: By the way, did you look where you were going?

A: What is this!

Q: This is Tuesday. Did you look?

A: Of course I looked. I always look. Who doesn't look? What am I?

Q: You don't mean to say you keep looking down on the ground as you walk along, do you?

A: Always.

Q: Head down, looking at the ground?

A: Of course not. I look, as everybody looks. Everybody looks where they are going. You know what I mean. You walk along, and out of the corner of your eye, you see where you are walking. You know that, Counselor. You know what I mean all right . . .

74

At length the city's lawyer gave it up. Enough was enough. The witness was not going to break; why make it worse? So he took his seat as he muttered to the witness, "You may step down."

And then it happened. The witness, in stepping down from the platform that holds the witness chair, tangled up his feet in some way and fell headlong across the floor, ending at the counsel table, passing before the startled gaze of the jurors like a jet out of control, and landing on his ear.

The judge, both counsel, the court officer and some of the jurors promptly examined the premises and found them to be in good order.

Whereupon the city's lawyer recalled the plaintiff to the stand:

Q: What made you fall just now?
A: What made me fall?
PLAINTIFF'S COUNSEL: I object, Your Honor. The question here is whether he fell on the night in question, not now.
CITY'S COUNSEL: Don't bother to rule, Your Honor; I withdraw the question. The witness may step down. Watch your step, sir!

Let us catch an earful of the summation. The city's lawyer:

Ladies and gentlemen of the jury: I am not going to bore you with a lot of talk. The City has claimed, from the very beginning, that there was nothing the matter with this sidewalk; that the plaintiff either dreamed about this alleged toe-trap, or was drunk or incapaci-

75

tated at the time he claims he fell into it. Maybe he was nearsighted. Come to think of it, I forgot to ask him about his vision. Perhaps he sees well, perhaps not.

I say to you that that sidewalk was in the same perfect condition as that witness stand!

I will admit I couldn't trip the witness. He was too clever for me, but trip he did; and it will be interesting to see whether he is going to sue the City for today's episode! Perhaps he will claim we should have had a red light there! Perhaps he will claim the judge should have helped him off the stand!

If you give this man one red cent for his toe-trap case I say you should pay him for his fall from the witness stand! I thank you!

It might be interesting to see how the poor plaintiff's lawyer handles this unfortunate affair on the summation. One would think there was just nothing to say, but this lawyer is going down fighting:

Members of the jury: *I* am not going to abandon my unfortunate client at this time. *I* am not going to abandon him, as my resourceful friend wants *you* to abandon him! No, I am going to see him through!

Some people are lucky and some are not. My client belongs to the second group. I think if he found himself in a department store and the lights went out he would be in the piano department.

On the other hand, my fortunate friend here belongs to the first group; he would probably find himself in the jewelry department — with the safe open.

My client tells a clean, honest, straightforward story, the story of a taxpayer who has been injured by the care-

lessness and recklessness and callousness of this municipality, and no one breaks him down, because he is
telling the truth! You can't beat the truth! Not even
my experienced friend here can get around the truth!

And then what happens? As you are about to compensate
him for his excruciating pain and suffering, he falls
off the witness stand!

No, ladies and gentlemen, I don't know what made this
unfortunate taxpayer, this family man, fall from that
witness stand; I don't know anything more about it
than you do! But I have a theory!

Perhaps he fell from that stand *because of the weakened
condition of his ankle, resulting from the fall into that
toe-trap!*

What does my civil-service friend think of *that?*

I can suggest another solution, too. Perhaps this unlucky
taxpayer, this war veteran, fell from that stand because
of one of the dizzy spells that he has been subject to
since that toe-trap accident.

Perhaps my learned friend's grueling, two-hour cross-
examination was too much for him.

You will remember, my client has never been in court
before. It is a strain to cope with a clever lawyer who
is trying to belittle you, to becloud your name and
your very integrity! Perhaps you would have fallen! I
myself might have fallen from that stand!

Think it over, ladies and gentlemen! I think you will
show more fairness than my comfortable friend, who
is working for the City and has nothing to worry about!

I thank you.

This jury has work to do and may not get home in
time for the late late show.

77

THE SCENE SHIFTERS

PEOPLE WHO think about suing often overdo it, and we can see this right from the files.

This particular man was Herman Ecks, aged twenty-seven. On a beautiful Sunday afternoon he took a trip to a nearby country club and went swimming in the pool. For the benefit of a ravishing redhead he tried a full gainer with a double twist, from the high board, and broke his arm.

An ambulance was called and he was rushed to the hospital where X rays were taken and revealed not only a broken arm but a fractured right wrist.

Before anyone had a chance to treat him he was seized with a brilliant idea and sneaked out of the hospital.

Back at his apartment, he telephoned a bosom friend and outlined the plan: "This can't miss, Beedle. Now look: for that swimming-pool thing I can't get a quarter from anybody. But if you saw me fall on the stairs in the house here — "

Ecks and Beedle went right over to another hospital in the vicinity of the apartment building and they said that Ecks fell down a flight of stairs. X rays were taken and showed the fractures suffered in the swimming pool.

They went to an attorney who, innocently enough, drew up the papers for a fifty-thousand-dollar lawsuit against the owner of the apartment building.

The flabbergasted owner turned it over to the insurance company, and they put the bloodhounds to work.

In jig time they got the goods on Herman, complete with hospital records, and took it to the District Attorney for prosecution. Herman was indicted and convicted, and

78

in the end confessed and received an appropriate sentence.

Which certainly indicates that one can be too enthusiastic about a lawsuit.

SUICIDE

IF YOU ARE going to sue someone you will have to say what he did — or failed to do — that caused you injury or damage. This file is about a man who committed suicide over a love problem and the lawsuit that resulted.

The problem was simple enough. This young man's girl had chosen another. It was a bitter blow and he decided to commit suicide. He turned on the five gas jets in his one-room apartment and locked all the doors and windows. The pilot light finally got to the gas and there was hell to pay. The man was hurled through the floor by the blast. The range was catapulted through a wall into the adjoining apartment. A waffle iron crashed through another wall into still another apartment.

When the smoke cleared away, seven persons were dead, including the despondent young man, and more than ten injured, and two apartment houses were wrecked.

79

The lawsuit: The widow of one of the dead tenants sued the landlord on the theory that he knew or should have known that Smith was trying to take his life and using means to do so which endangered other tenants; despite that knowledge, he did nothing to control him, or to evict him; he failed to report it to the police or city authorities or to take any steps to abate the danger.

The plaintiff asked $350,000.

As of now the plaintiff has lost the first round of this lawsuit, but it is on appeal and a decision is pending.

The actual testimony in this case is not readily available, but it might be that the despondent young man had a number of conversations with other tenants in the building, *including the superintendent,* about his troubles, and probably expressed his intention to end it all, and, that this information should have trickled back to the owner of the building and that he should have taken steps at once to prevent it.

This theory would certainly seem to hold water. If the owner of a building has information that the building is in danger, he should certainly close up his building or take some steps to abate the danger, or at least warn the tenants that there is a dangerous condition, and give them a chance to get out or remain at their peril. If he knew about the young man's wild plan he had no right to gamble on whether the youth would change his mind.

And the landlord cannot say, "Maybe my superintendent knew about it, but I didn't," because the superintendent is in his employ and this makes him responsible for all matters connected with the building.

Of course, it might be argued that if this information was kicking around the building so persistently, the tenants should all have had wind of it in no time and acted on their own.

80

So it all winds up in court, and if it does nothing else, it gives the jurors terrific alibis for coming home late.

PROVING A STORY

SINCE IT IS the plaintiff who must prove his case, it would be well to see how one goes about *proving* a story.

A good way to see just what proof is would be this: You place a number of things on a table — a loaf of bread, a bottle of beer, a tin of sardines, a tomato, a jar of Danish mushrooms in wine sauce, and a bottle of Mother Fletcher's Tonic. What have you? Groceries.

Now, in the same way, you place upon the table a letter, a torn envelope, an old shoe, a machine gun (monogramed) and a losing ticket from the third race. What have you? *Proof.* That is, they are *proof* when considered collectively. Taken separately they are merely items of *evidence,* but if they fit together well and are strong enough to stand up as a unit, they are *proof.* It is exactly like a brick wall: the bricks are the *evidence;* the wall is the *proof.* To make sure: if the bricks stick together strongly enough you have proved that you have a wall.

In a trial, if you throw enough bricks around, you may finally *prove* something. Of course, you may prove that you're a mental case, but that is another subject.

If you can't prove a thing one way, you might prove it in another. You take the stand and say you sent the defendant a letter on December 12th. He denies it. He says he never received a letter from you or anybody else. You can prove it by secondary proof. You testify: "I wrote this man a letter on December 12th, 1957. I signed it. I put it in an envelope, which I addressed to him. I put a stamp on the envelope, also my return address. I deposited the letter in a mailbox on the southeast corner of Fifth Avenue and Forty-fifth Street and never got it back."

There is a very strong presumption in law that a letter, properly addressed and mailed, reaches its destination and, for the moment, you have *proved* that you sent the letter and he got it.

In other words, if the things you say make people believe your story you have *proved* it. If you can make your wife believe you came in last night before midnight and not at four A.M. you have certainly proved it. It doesn't matter whether you merely talked fast, or showed her a break-away clock or last year's calendar or what. If she believes you, you have proved it.

BUT —

Now ABOUT this burden of proof — it shifts. This is tricky, but hang on: The plaintiff has the burden of proving *his* story, but when the defendant's turn comes, the defendant has the burden of proving *his* story.

About this letter. At this point we believe the plaintiff sent it and the defendant received it. Now the defendant gets a chance to prove that he never did get it. The only way he can actually prove that is to show that it is still in the dead-letter section of the post office, to get the postman to admit burning it for spite, or to show that at around that time he was on the baseball team at San Quentin.

True, we hear of letters delivered twenty-two years late, but you cannot prove that until it is finally delivered, and who will wait twenty-two years for you?

Sometimes your only way of proving a thing happened may be to show that it *could* have happened.

If, for example, you have told the jury that the reason you knew the murder occurred at six-fifteen was that on that evening you had just finished playing the "Minute Waltz" in thirty seconds and wondered what had slowed you down and so had occasion to look at the clock, the jury is going to look at you askance if not worse; but if your lawyer suddenly wheels in a piano and you play the "Minute Waltz" in thirty seconds the jury is likely to regard you respectfully from there on. You have lent credence to your story, you have made it believable.

In an actual case some years ago a lady sued the manufacturers of a certain facial cream for personal injuries. She claimed it ruined her skin. She said that ten minutes after she put the stuff on it nearly took the skin off her face and generally made a mess of it; that even her hands were burned, handling this cream. As she sat there testifying, she looked pretty good, but she said the thing had been a while back and had mostly healed up, but while it lasted it was dreadful, and she had to go into hiding for a long time. The plaintiff was doing all right up to there.

But the defendant's attorney was a frustrated actor at heart. He asked the permission of the court to send the court officer to the nearest drugstore for a jar of this cream, and when it was brought in, he smeared his face with it and got it all over his hands — got some of it on his blue suit too because he was something of a slob.

But he continued to conduct the case for the remainder of the day with all this cream on his face, to show how harmless it actually was.

The jury got home early, after a verdict against the lady.

Of course, there were a lot of objections, to the effect that what was true of one jar might not necessarily be true of another jar. But it was a great demonstration and the jury loved it.

CONTRIBUTORY NEGLIGENCE

THIS IS A thing a plaintiff must be careful about. If you are guilty of contributory negligence it means that you have helped in some way to cause the accident, and if you do that you can't win your case, no matter how negligent the defendant may have been.

Take this lady with the facial cream. If, after opening the jar, fresh from the drugstore, she had decided it was too thick and wanted to thin it out a bit, poured a jigger of turpentine in and stirred, she would have been guilty of contributory negligence and the lawyer would not have had the opportunity to ham it up as he did, because the plaintiff's case would have collapsed early.

In another kind of a case, if you undertake to read a comic book as you cross the street backward and a car comes along at eighty miles an hour and makes contact, you may not collect a quarter.

True, eighty miles an hour is on the speedy side, but your conduct was a little offbeat too.

This does not mean that it is *impossible* for you to win. It means that the court will charge the jury that they must take into consideration your unusual method of crossing the street and that if they believe it helped cause the accident, they must find against you.

They might.

This does not mean that the motorist could not be locked up for reckless driving. He might have been a drunk driver at that (*see* chapter on Booze and Your Future).

FROM LITTLE ACORNS

THIS IS NOT a legal term, but it is good for a plaintiff to remember that some pretty big things grow out of little acorns, and the files prove it.

Everybody knows about the little monster who ran whimpering to his mother with two beautiful black eyes, all cuts and bruises. The mother was aghast and cross-examined: "How did it start?" And the delinquent snapped back: "The whole thing started when he hit me back."

Now, in this file the man was insured for $5,000, and one of the clauses in his policy provided for double indemnity in case of accident; that is to say, if he died by reason of an accident, his widow was to get $10,000.

The man died, and the insurance company refused to pay the double indemnity, claiming the death was not an accident within the meaning of the law.

At the trial, the following facts were brought out:

On a balmy summer evening our man sauntered into a tavern up in the country and stopped at the bar. He

85

ordered a double Scotch, with a single for a chaser, then another, and a couple for the road.

Then he looked around the room and found out he didn't like the man standing next to him. He muttered something to this man and shoved him. The stranger protested, but our man still didn't like him and invited him outside. The stranger said he was comfortable where he stood.

Our man shoved him through the door and in a moment they were doing one of those John Wayne things all over the place.

The stranger finally landed one right on the button. Our man fell back and his head struck an iron fixture at the entrance to the tavern, killing him instantly.

It was the widow's contention that the whole affair was plainly an accident, and she wanted the double payment, $10,000.

The company claimed that while the matter was indeed unfortunate, it was not an accident in the eyes of the law.

The courts upheld the company's contention, even on appeal, and held, in substance, that it was not an accident, because the dead man was the aggressor; he had started the fight.

This decision stuck, and the widow received only $5,000.

MURDER AND SELF-DEFENSE

THIS *aggressor* business is important not only to a plaintiff but to anyone who is running around with loose notions about self-defense.

To kill in self-defense there must be immediate danger

of death or of serious bodily harm. The danger doesn't even have to be real, so long as you believe it to be real. In a sudden brawl, the party threatened must back away as far as possible with safety before taking the life of the attacker. But the big thing is this: If in any way you *start* the brawl or the argument, or *provoke* it — look out! It won't be self-defense, it will be *murder*.

To restate this (because of its importance):

If you go into a diner for a cup of coffee and say to the man on the adjoining stool, "Mister, it's people like you give this country a bad name," and he suddenly pulls a murderous knife and goes after you — you are *not* defending yourself, you are merely finishing up a little transaction that you initiated and you are strictly on your own. (*See* chapter on Silence and Longevity — under the subheading Your Mouth and What It Means to You.)

THE REPORT

YOU MIGHT be badly injured on a train, say, and decide to sue the railroad. The decision to sue may not occur to you until you get home, or even at some later time, but while you are on the train, and as close to the time of the accident as possible, there is something you'd better do: report the happening to the conductor, together with your name, of course, so that he has an official record of it. Otherwise your lawsuit will be an "unreported case" —

not very highly regarded anywhere, because if you were badly injured, people would have come running, someone would have called the conductor, he would have taken your name and the details and thus created a solid background for your case. If you don't report it, you look like this on the witness stand:.

Q: Madam, you say that as the train roared around the bend at this excessive speed, there was a sudden lurch and you were thrown clear across the aisle?

A: Exactly.

Q: Your head struck the water cooler near the rear platform?

A: Yes, sir.

Q: Nearly cracking it open — your head, that is?

A: Yes, sir.

Q: Rendering you unconscious?

A: Yes, sir.

Q: And bleeding?

A: Oh, yes.

Q: Profusely?

A: Yes, sir.

Q: The train was crowded?

A: Yes, sir.

Q: You don't know how long you lay there, but you finally came to, brushed yourself off, went through the car looking for your handbag and glasses and returned to your seat?

A: That's right.

Q: Without saying a word to anyone?

A: What do you mean? I didn't know anyone on the train. They were strangers.

Q: I mean the conductor. He was a stranger too. Is that why you didn't mention it to him?

A: He wasn't there. He was in another car.

Q: All the way to Denver? This happened at Pittsburgh!

A: Really, I don't know. I have been all confused since this accident.

Q: Isn't it strange that no one volunteered to help you as you lay unconscious at the water cooler?

A: I can't explain about other people; I can only tell what happened.

Q: Weren't you in the way when someone came for a drink? Wouldn't someone have tripped over you?

A: Nobody tripped.

By this time you are probably ready to throw your own case out of court.

On the other hand, you can report the happening promptly and correctly and still make another big mistake. If, right after the accident, you go through the car and get the name and address of everyone in sight, check the dimensions, measurements and distances and write the thing up like an engineering survey, the jury may get the impression that you couldn't have been hurt very seriously and be so busy and efficient.

It is a delicate matter and must be handled with a good deal of common sense.

THE PHOTOGRAPH

IF YOU EVER run into a character who explains things with his fists, and he knocks your nose out of shape, closes both your eyes, dents your forehead, puffs up your lips and alters your cheekbones, you may feel you want to sue him civilly for, say, fifty thousand dollars.

In such a case, a good photograph of your face with all these alterations would be a handy thing to show the jury and might not only save you a lot of time on the witness stand but might make the jury feel that fifty thousand is not enough.

A word, however, about the photograph. It should be dated and have on it the name of the photographer, even if a friend or relative, because they might ask you to produce him in court for cross-examination, to find out about possible trick shots, or retouching or the like.

In any type of case where a photograph can be produced it is always effective and makes an excellent witness, whether it is a broken stair tread, a defective sidewalk, a dark hallway or a demolished automobile.

Getting back to your face for a moment, your case doesn't come up for many months, and by the time you take the witness stand your face has healed nicely and you look beautiful. Well, it takes a little imagination to believe that those classic features could have been so badly mangled as you describe, so the photograph helps tremendously.

I'VE GOT WITNESSES!

GOOD FOR YOU, but who is going to believe them? It depends upon who these witnesses are.

If a man brings his wife to court to corroborate his story, the jury might not pay too much attention to her testimony because she is the man's wife. What wife will not say her husband is telling the truth? In a courtroom, that is.

A brother will not help a case much; neither will a sister, because of the relationship. Even a close friend has at least one strike on him.

Strangers make the best witnesses, because it can be argued that they are disinterested in the outcome of the lawsuit.

Why, then, are these relatives put upon the stand? Because it must be done. Let us see why.

Suppose you come home from the office of an evening and hear this:

91

"Don't get too comfortable there, Harry; we're going out tonight, you know."

"We're what!"

"O-U-T, lover; the Browns', for dinner and bridge, so don't get too cozy there. In fact, we'll just make it. Up, boy, up — "

Well, this is plain talk, and straight from the chain of command, so in no time you are on the way to the Browns.

There are twelve for dinner. Things go along smoothly enough, despite the presence of her no-good brother Borword and a couple of other characters.

But after dinner, when everyone is sort of draped about the living room, Borword sounds off, which figures. This time it is on his favorite subject, same as last time — or any other time, for that matter:

"I've said it before and I'll say it again, it's disgusting, is what it is. A married man, in this part of the world anyway, hasn't a chance. In fact he doesn't rate the title of Man any longer. He's just about nothing, is what he is. Pick up a magazine — you'll see a man with an apron on — a lace apron — doing the dishes. Turn on the Thing — you'll see a commercial, with a man scrubbing the floor and raving about the fun of doing it with Floreslop instead of those other harsh compounds which are so rough on the hands a man can't hold the cooking pot steady — "

An unnatural quiet prevails. It is an ominous moment. In a far corner sits Mrs. Migrayne, a large, powerful woman with a compelling resemblance to a prison matron — a *chief* prison matron. She nudges her husband, a little pipsqueak of a man, and whispers hoarsely, "Henry, are you going to let that unmarried monster say these disgusting things! Where is your backbone! Speak up and tell him off — " she looks at him sharply — "or do you, by

92

some unlucky coincidence, *agree* with his obscene ravings!!"

Well, Henry is startled, but he has had the Word, which is more official than a notarized death warrant. He edges over toward the center ring. But Borword has only started. He takes a breath and goes on:

"The payoff was just the other night. I saw a movie where this little eight-year-old boy had a nightmare and screamed, and his young parents rushed in, and the father comforted the boy and said, 'Get into your clothes, Son, and we'll go for a walk; buy a soda.' *Do you know what that child said?*"

The quiet in the room is like a vacuum. Borword goes on.

"The child said: 'Is it all right, Mom?'"

"Well, if that isn't the living end of everything — "

You are fascinated as you watch what follows. Little Henry Migrayne, darting a quick glance at his towering wife for a last official O.K., steps up and taps Borword on the chest.

"Look here, Borword, I resent your remarks. You single fellows are all alike, always sounding off about marriage as if it were some kind of a *prison* — " Henry darts another look toward the corner and shudders. He braces his narrow shoulders and continues: "The actual fact is that you people are envious of a married man, and a family, and a home. And another thing: the truth is that a woman wouldn't *have* you people, and so you're always sniping at the fellows who have the luck to find the right party and get married, because you're not man enough — "

These last two words turn out to be unfortunate. Borword, without a word, lands a clean right to Henry's nose, sending him straight into the grand piano, which clamps shut and hides everything but his toes.

93

Now this is no way to treat a little guy, and besides, it is your golden opportunity to have a go at Borword.

Well, in no time at all, chairs are flying, some pretty serious damage is done to faces and noses, eyes are gouged out, hair pulled by the handful, Brown's beautiful sitting room is a shambles, and after all the charges and counter-charges are straightened out in the criminal court, you bring a civil suit against Brown, who threw you out of the window because you were related to Borword.

Well, after you have told your story, your lawyer *must* call your wife to the stand, not so much to show that her version agrees with yours, for of course it will, but because if he doesn't call her, the other lawyer will say something like this on summation:

Members of the jury, there is something peculiar about this case, mighty peculiar. Here is a lady who was in the room at the time, right beside her husband. Why doesn't she take the stand? Why didn't she testify? I'll tell you why! Because she doesn't dare! Husband or no husband, she knows he started the whole thing and she doesn't want to commit perjury — and I don't blame her, ladies and gentlemen. Indeed, I admire her for it. I also admire the brother-in-law and sister-in-law. In fact, I admire everybody but this asocial plaintiff who, given one drink and a captive audience, airs his warped views — in the very home of his host.

And you lose.

Sometimes the relationship of a witness doesn't hurt too much. Occasionally, in cases involving a number of witnesses, they are directed to remain out of the courtroom until called. They are called, one by one, to give their versions. If they survive the cross-examination, their testimony may be valuable.

94

Suppose you have just told your story of an automobile collision, and your lawyer turns you over to opposing counsel for cross-examination. This ordeal may take an hour or more, during which you will be asked many questions concerning measurements, distances, conversations, the colors of traffic lights, the number of other vehicles upon the road, and so on.

One by one, your wife, brother-in-law and sister-in-law will be asked practically the same questions.

If the answers tally, your witnesses may have helped you, and your lawyer will argue like this when he sums up to the jury:

Ladies and gentlemen: You have heard our witnesses. Did you notice that my very capable opponent, with all his experience in these matters, failed utterly to break them down? And not for want of trying, I assure you. Did you notice how logically their stories fitted together, and how they withstood the grueling cross-examination of my learned friend? There is a reason for this, members of the jury, a very simple reason: They were telling the truth, all of them. You can't beat the truth!

And you win.

WATCH OUT

IF THE STORIES fit too well, there is trouble.

If you have testified the boulevard was forty-eight feet wide, and your wife says forty-eight and your brother-in-law and his wife say forty-eight — *forty-eight* is going to be your unlucky number.

If you have said the defendant wore a blue suit with

red stripes an eighth of an inch apart, that the traffic light was three feet five inches from the curb, and your witnesses back you up exactly one hundred per cent, the other lawyer will put it this way:

Ladies and gentlemen: My old law professor used to tell us to watch the little things. He used to say "Watch those little things; they will show you the way; they will tell you where the truth is." Did you notice how this big, happy family agreed? Did you observe how their interesting stories dovetailed to the very syllable? Did you see that there wasn't a quarter of an inch of difference among them? Not a red stripe? I leave it to you whether they rehearsed this little play, down to the last detail! Is it humanly possible for four stories to agree to the letter? Can't you just see them, in some quiet corner, putting this thing together, shoring up the discrepancies? Of course you can! I thank you.

And you lose.

4

THE PEOPLE IN
THE COURTROOM

THE JUDGE

THE JUDGE is supposed to sit up there, in a jury case anyway, and act as an umpire, because all the facts are judged by the jury. The witnesses testify, the lawyers argue, object and declaim, the judge sees that nobody comes to blows and explains certain points of law to the jurors so they may know what to ignore and what to wrestle with. No one, and that includes the judge, is permitted to interfere with the jury's right and duty to decide the facts.

Theoretically, that is.

Actually, however, it doesn't always work out that way and the judge gets his oar in to the extent that you are a dead duck or a made man, as the case may be.

97

This is because the judge is only human, despite the snide rumors one hears from time to time, and is subject to the same idiosyncrasies, prejudices, weaknesses, moods and emotions that brought you to court in the first place. Many judges succeed in rising above these human traits — to the point, in fact, of being inhuman. Some, however, are just plain human, and that can be a very lucky or unlucky break for you.

For example, there is the *defendant-minded* judge. This judge hates plaintiffs; wouldn't believe a plaintiff on a stack of affidavits, even if they were notarized. Now, if you are a plaintiff you certainly wandered into the wrong courtroom, or picked the wrong day or something. He can cook your goose in more ways than you could find in an international cookbook. He can make frequent interruptions while your lawyer is trying to make you comfortable and gently elicit your story. He can turn on you suddenly and direct you to speak up. He can make a face just as you have reached the high point of your narrative. He can swivel in his chair — with this face — so that the jury can have a look at it . . . Well, let's watch him. (You are testifying:)

Q: Mr. Tufluk, you always take this route on your way home?

A: Yes, sir.

THE COURT: Always?

THE WITNESS: Well, yes, sir.

THE COURT: Speak up, sir, speak up. Is there something secret about this case?

THE WITNESS: Yes, sir.

THE COURT: What!

THE WITNESS: Why, Your Honor, I mean yes to the question.

THE COURT: Now, look here, Mr. Witness, we're not going to be confused; you can depend on that. Now, why do you always take this route home? What is so special about this route? You certainly didn't sit up nights planning —

PLAINTIFF's COUNSEL: Your Honor, may I respectfully —

THE COURT: You may not. We're going to get to the bottom —

PLAINTIFF's COUNSEL: Why, Your Honor, this was just a casual question leading up to —

THE COURT: I have an idea what it is leading up to, sir; you may depend on it. Now, if you have an objection to the court's question —

PLAINTIFF's COUNSEL: I don't even know what it is.

THE COURT: Then you're not paying attention. I'll give you an objection, and throw in an exception. Now, let's get on with it.

PLAINTIFF's COUNSEL: Where are we at this point, Your Honor? I mean —

THE COURT: Look here, you called this witness. Now get on with your examination — if you have any.

Q: Mr. Tufluk, let's get right to the injuries —

THE COURT: If any.

PLAINTIFF's COUNSEL: Your Honor, with the deepest respect I object —

THE COURT: What do you object to now?

PLAINTIFF's COUNSEL: I object to Your Honor's remark, "if any."

THE COURT: There has been no testimony thus far about any injuries, Counselor. Is that correct?

PLAINTIFF's COUNSEL: Yes, sir, but —

THE COURT: Then "if any" would certainly be a logical addition to your question; improve it, I would say. Now, Counselor, we must get on with this case; we have a great many other cases to follow and we are wasting the taxpayers' money with all this bickering.

PLAINTIFF'S COUNSEL: I must say for the record, Your Honor, I have not been bickering. I have a duty to my client —

THE COURT: I am losing my patience with you, sir. Your zeal is commendable, but you do not listen well. I did not say *whose* bickering. I said *this* bickering, and the reporter will bear me out. Now, let's get on with it.

Let us skip the painful details of the next seventy-three pages and look in on you at a later point in the trial. You are still on the stand. Dying, but still in there. You are being cross-examined by the lawyer for the other side:

Q: Mr. Tufluk, tell us how you spent the three days preceding this affair.

A: Three days?

Q: The three days preceding.

A: Well, three days! It is difficult to remember exactly —

THE COURT: *What-was-that!*

THE WITNESS: He is asking me to remember exactly —

THE COURT: And he has a perfect right to ask you, sir. If I recall correctly, you remembered *exactly* how many times you talked with Skurvy; you remembered *exactly* where he struck you, and how many times, and with what degree of force; you remembered *exactly* what was said. Now this attorney, who has a duty to his client, sir, wishes to know how you spent the three days. Answer the question.

PLAINTIFF'S COUNSEL: Your Honor, may my client have a glass of water?

THE COURT: By all means, if it will help him to answer the question —

100

PLAINTIFF'S COUNSEL: Now Your Honor is implying —

THE COURT: Look here, young man, you are treading on thin ice. Do I make myself clear?

PLAINTIFF'S COUNSEL: But a glass of water —

THE COURT: No one is denying him water. And he could have had it when he was remembering all those other things, too; didn't seem to need it then. If he needs it now, let him have it. We'll do anything to get answers to these questions and get on to these other cases. The taxpayers —

PLAINTIFF'S COUNSEL: Yes, Your Honor, I know.

THE COURT: Watch it, young man . . .

If your goose is not done to a golden brown by this time, don't be impatient; our friend is about to charge the jury:

THE COURT: Ladies and gentlemen of the jury, we have been here for three days now [a slow, thirty-degree turn in your direction with a baleful glare] and we have heard the testimony of all the witnesses.

It now becomes your duty to say who shall prevail. You must say whether you believe the story of this — this *plaintiff* [back to you again] or that of the defendant, Mr. Skurvy, who resists this claim, as he has a perfect right to do.

Now, as to the story of the plaintiff. I have heard a lot of stories in my time, but this plaintiff wants you to believe [a touch of suppressed emotion] that he received these injuries in the manner described by him, and it is your solemn duty, indeed your privilege, to examine his story with the utmost care, that true justice may be done between these parties —

Nineteen pages of this, with some of the most subtle

101

and eloquent bits of stage business this side of a proscenium, till at the end your attorney rises to make the usual exceptions to the charge:

PLAINTIFF'S COUNSEL: I respectfully except to Your Honor's continual glances at my client —

THE COURT: Be careful, sir.

PLAINTIFF'S COUNSEL: I also take exception to Your Honor's repeated references to his "story," whereas in referring to the defendant you always speak of his "testimony."

THE COURT: Your exception will be noted, young man, but do you undertake to confine this court to the use of one monotonous noun when there are so many in the dictionary? Really, sir!

PLAINTIFF'S COUNSEL: I respectfully except to Your Honor's remarks that you "have heard a lot of stories" in your time.

THE COURT: Do you question that as a fact, Counselor?

PLAINTIFF'S COUNSEL: No, Your Honor, but there is the implication —

THE COURT: Young man, throughout this protracted trial the thought has occurred to me that perhaps you were deliberately trying the patience of this court. I dismissed it each time as unworthy of a member of the bar. Please do not revive such an unpleasant thought. There will be no mistrial here, sir, I assure you.

PLAINTIFF'S COUNSEL: I object to that remark, sir. Respectfully.

THE COURT: What remark?

PLAINTIFF'S COUNSEL: About a mistrial. It implies —

THE COURT: Counselor, these jurors look intelligent enough to me. I do not think they need an interpreter to supply these running commentaries about implica-

102

tions. Now have you any further exceptions to this charge?

PLAINTIFF'S COUNSEL: [You've got a pretty spunky lawyer here.] I have not even *begun,* sir.

THE COURT: Then I suggest you begin at once and conclude as quickly as possible.

PLAINTIFF'S COUNSEL: I ask Your Honor to charge this jury that they must give equal consideration to the testimony of both sides.

THE COURT: That goes without saying, young man. Are you inferring that these jurors are ignorant of the very foundation of our democracy, the very —

PLAINTIFF'S COUNSEL: I object to that remark, Your Honor, as positively inflammatory, and I move for a mistrial.

THE COURT: Your objection is overruled and your motion is denied. The only thing inflamed around here, sir, is you, and I suggest that you quench it and move along here; the taxpayers —

A reader might say at this point: Surely twelve jurors don't go for all this, hook, line and sinker? Well, let us put an ear, with the court officer, to the locked door of the jury room:

JUROR NO. 3: How do you like that sonofabitch?

JUROR NO. 5: Who are you referring to?

JUROR NO. 7: Whom.

JUROR NO. 5: That's what I said.

JUROR NO. 3: Who else!

THE FOREMAN: Ladies and gentlemen, let's get organized here. I am the foreman, as you know. Let's analyze this case.

JUROR NO. 3: I say there's nothing to analyze; let's give

103

the plaintiff the full amount, plus costs and interest.

JUROR NO. 7: Are you crazy, mister? How did you arrive at a deal like that? Are you forgetting about the testimony of the police officers? And the hospital intern? Why —

JUROR NO. 3: I'm not forgettin' about nuthin'. We're supposed to deal out justice here, is what I always been told, and as far as I am concerned the only justice possible here is to show that sonofabitch he didn't get away with it. Furthermore —

THE FOREMAN: Pardon me, sir. I didn't get your name —

JUROR NO. 3: Bludd.

THE FOREMAN: We will overlook the fact that you have called the judge a sonofabitch —

JUROR NO. 9: Why overlook it? If ever I saw a sonofabitch, there was one in action.

THE FOREMAN: Madam! Will you just let me talk to Mr. Bludd here a minute? I was about to tell him to watch his language.

JUROR NO. 11: Well, tell him to watch my language too, because I agree with the lady, only sonofabitch is not strong enough. I am sure there is a stronger word. It will come to me in a moment.

THE FOREMAN: Now, just a minute, all of you. I have a right to demand order here. You three people are not running this show. If you think the judge is a — well, whatever you think about the judge has no bearing here. We are dealing with a lawsuit. Now, personally, I don't like the plaintiff's case.

JUROR NO. 3: I don't either; wouldn't give you two cents for it. But that judge is a sonofabitch and what other way can we let him know it?

JUROR NO. 11: Exactly. I think the plaintiff's case is weak too. But that judge — by the way, that word just came to me — he is a *dirty* sonofabitch. I knew it would come to me if —

THE FOREMAN: Order here now! I think this kind of talk is un-American and —

JUROR NO. 3: *Just* a minute, Buster; who you calling a Communist!

JUROR NO. 7: Whom.

JUROR NO. 3: Shut up. Now, you over there, Foreman or not, you're getting a punch in the mouth and it's no use hiding behind this lady —

JUROR NO. 11: Wait for me, pal, he's getting two punches in the mouth; I'm no Communist either —

Many readers might say at this point that you really have nothing to worry about, because if you lose this case, the law gives you the right to take an appeal and correct all these judicial errors in one fell swoop. It sure does — *but*:

1. Appeals cost money.
2. They cost a lot of money.
3. You must buy the reporter's minutes — that is, every word uttered in the trial. This highly skilled, official record can cost anywhere from five or ten dollars to five hundred or ten hundred dollars, depending upon the number of pages. (With this judge every other question took three or four pages instead of one line.) You have to put up that money right away. (*If* you win in the higher court you might get it back, but in the meantime you'll have to get it up.) In many states a number of copies of the entire record must be *printed* because the higher court won't look at typing. They just won't. Just for fun, run out and get a quotation on seven hundred pages of printing. Fourteen copies. Good paper.

105

4. There are other disbursements.

5. The lawyer won't work up a scholarly appeal for nothing.

6. Some lawyers are not elephants and won't work for peanuts.

7. After you lay out all this money, it takes a dog's age to perfect the appeal and get a decision.

8. You may lose again.

9. Judges in the higher court are human too.

10. You can take a further appeal.

11. How silly can you get?

But there is a tiny ray of hope for you yet: in the case just concluded things are not going too well in the jury room; it may end in a bloody free-for-all and result in a mistrial, which will give you your big chance to start all over again. But don't ask for a change of venue because judges are human all over.

There is the *plaintiff-minded* judge, and it should not come as a surprise that he leans the other way; he hates defendants and will do whatever he can to make this clear. He can do plenty:

PLAINTIFF'S COUNSEL: Your Honor, I represent this plaintiff, the young woman who was injured. May we proceed at this time?

THE COURT: By all means, Counselor. We do not keep plaintiffs waiting in this court. People who are injured have a right —

DEFENDANT'S COUNSEL: I object to that, Your Honor; I respectfully object to Your Honor's remark; it goes without saying that *both* sides have a right to be heard.

THE COURT: Counselor, did you flunk Good Manners And

106

Ethics in law school? In my day they taught us *never* to interrupt the court.

DEFENDANT'S COUNSEL: I know, but Your Honor is getting me off to a flying start here! These remarks at the outset —

THE COURT: Just take care, sir, that you do not make it a flying *finish*. Now let us get along here. This poor young plaintiff must be tired. Officer, bring the young lady a glass of water — and let her sit in this armchair until she is called. Easy there. Someone, help the lady over —

DEFENDANT'S COUNSEL: Your Honor! Really, sir! The injuries here are bruised elbows! They have nothing to do with a grown woman walking over to a chair! And she has not asked for water. This jury is going to think —

THE COURT: Young man, if *you* choose to go through life without the common courtesies, that is *your* affair, deplorable though it may be. But I, sir, will not be told how to treat a lady! And a plaintiff, at that! I mean, there are injuries claimed here —

DEFENDANT'S COUNSEL: Elbows!

THE COURT: Patience, sir. The case has just begun. Now let's get on with it.

Q: Miss Eiful, tell us what happened.

A: Well, I was entering this department store and there was this big crowd and no guards —

THE COURT: *No guards!* Do you mean to say they had no guards there to regulate these crowds?

THE WITNESS: That's right, Judge. No guards.

THE COURT: Proceed, Counselor. Let's get to the bottom of this! The very bottom!

DEFENDANT'S COUNSEL: I object to that, Your Honor.

107

THE COURT: You object to finding out what happened here?

DEFENDANT'S COUNSEL: Not at all. I object to Your Honor's picturesque phrases, and Your Honor's fine timing and —

THE COURT: Careful, sir!

Eighty-two pages later:

PLAINTIFF'S COUNSEL: Your Honor, may we have the young lady show her leg to the jury, so they can see —

THE COURT: By all means. Better than a thousand words, as the saying goes.

DEFENDANT'S COUNSEL: Over my dead —

THE COURT: What is that, sir?

DEFENDANT'S COUNSEL: Does Your Honor mean to say you're going to allow a burlesque show here before this jury?

THE COURT: Counselor, I have been patient about your remarks concerning the Court, but be careful about this young lady and your talk about burlesque shows —

DEFENDANT'S COUNSEL: But her leg! What on earth has her leg to do with her elbows!

THE COURT: We don't know yet, and we are not going to deprive the jury —

DEFENDANT'S COUNSEL: But there are no injuries claimed to the leg!

THE COURT: True. Perhaps counsel wishes to compare the texture of the skin of the elbows —

DEFENDANT'S COUNSEL: But, Your Honor, this is an all-male jury, and your Honor is fully aware —

THE COURT: All gentlemen, I think, sir, and fully capable of behaving —

DEFENDANT'S COUNSEL: But Your Honor knows there is a natural —

THE COURT: Do you seek to regulate the phenomena of physiology, sir, as well as the conduct of the Court and the witnesses? Sometimes, Counselor, I get a feeling you go too far! You may have an exception. Here, somebody, help the lady —

Finally the case gets to the jury room, and it is just as well the poor defendant's lawyer can't hear what's going on up there:

JUROR NO. 2: I'll say one thing for that judge, he's a gentleman!

JUROR NO. 4: He's a phony!

JUROR NO. 2: Careful, sir!

JUROR NO. 4: See? He's got *you* talking like that!

JUROR NO. 2: How do you mean?

JUROR NO. 4: Don't you see? The pretty dame got the best of him.

JUROR NO. 7: Well, I don't mind telling you men she got the best of me too, as far as that goes!

JUROR NO. 9: Me too! Put me down on her side!

JUROR NO. 11: I'm a gentleman too. Let's take a vote.

THE FOREMAN: Now just a minute here. Is this a court of law or is it a popularity contest? We're supposed to —

JUROR NO. 10: Wait a minute, friend. What's wrong with a popularity contest? It's a good old American custom!

THE FOREMAN: We're not dealing with American customs here —

JUROR NO. 10: We ain't? Well, you just try to ring in any other kind of custom here and see what happens! American customs are good enough for *me*!

THE FOREMAN: American or not — the point is —

JUROR NO. 8: Look, mister, I don't like your attitude! Not one bit! Hey fellas! Anybody here like this man's attitude? He's against American customs —

109

Well, in no time at all there is a unanimous verdict for the little lady with the elbows, the foreman having changed his vote on the first ballot.

There is the strictly neutral judge, who hates both plaintiffs *and* defendants. He is mean throughout, with only an occasional breather, to renew his energies. If you get into step with this breather and can establish some kind of a cycle and testify in and out of it, you can do pretty well.

There is the bored judge, and you can do pretty well here too if he doesn't step on your punch line with a yawn.

Before leaving our judicial friends, it might be the better part of discretion to point out that a heartening number of patient, humane and scholarly gentlemen grace the bench and are a credit to our judicial system.

So, as the fellow says, lots of luck.

THE LAWYER

IF YOU GET mixed up with the law, as a plaintiff or a defendant, or if you're thinking about taking in a business partner or signing an important contract or buying a building or getting a divorce or taking any step involving the law, you need a lawyer. Make no mistake about it; the youngest and most inexperienced lawyer is infinitely better than a layman in these matters, just as the newest hospital intern is far better than a do-it-yourself deal when you're reeling with symptoms.

Yet there are an amazing number of people at large who will undertake the most important legal matters without consulting a lawyer, and wind up in court with

110

their lives, liberties or life's savings in jeopardy. This is probably because people are human.

It is difficult to believe, but contracts involving tremendous sums of money have been drawn by laymen wishing to save the expense of legal talent. Put it this way: If you can draw your own contract you can take out your own gall stones, which would make you a good all-around man.

It would appear to be a simple matter. A contract is merely the meeting of two minds on a given proposition. Two intelligent people should be able to put down on paper what they have agreed to do for each other.

But somehow it doesn't work out. Let us take a simple case:

Lyman Legree wants to hire Sherwood Shurk to work for him as a salesman for fifty dollars a week, plus one per cent commission.

Shurk can't afford a lawyer and Legree is conservative. So they meet at Legree's office and draw a contract: salesman, fifty dollars a week, one per cent commission. What more do they need? They write it out and sign it.

111

Now the fun begins. Shurk finds he can't live on fifty a week, plus one per cent, what with a wife and five children and a bum for a brother-in-law. So he takes on another line on the side. Lyman isn't going to like that.

Lyman finds he is paying Shurk too much money, what with one per cent and all, so he looks at the contract and finds it says: "One per cent commission on *sales*."

But it doesn't say anything about repeat orders. So he deducts the three St. Louis accounts. Shurk isn't going to like that.

Shurk doesn't, and to get even, he refuses to sweep the floor in the morning. There is nothing in the contract about that.

Legree will not stand for this, so he discontinues the one percent altogether, because nowhere in the contract does it say *when* the one per cent is payable.

Matters go from bad to worse and the first thing you know Legree and Shurk are in court, explaining the thing to a jury.

The contract is badly drawn; it is full of holes; and so the jury must listen to a few million words from the parties.

If Shurk makes a good impression, he will win; if Legree can disguise his sinister character well enough, *he* may win; and it becomes a battle of personalities — a question of who looks better, talks better, walks better, and stands up better under cross-examination, because there is nothing to go by except the stories of the two parties, their paper being worthless.

But if this is going to be the result of their homemade contract — an appearance in court and a long trial — they need not have drawn a contract at all; they might have been better off without one.

If the contract had been drawn by an experienced

attorney, with all possible contingencies provided for, the chances are that Shurk would still be selling Legree's goods and Legree would still be paying the one per cent, for there would be no loopholes in the contract.

It is, of course, possible that even a lawyer may leave out something, but in that case it would mean merely one item to be considered by a jury, and easily disposed of.

It is important to get a good lawyer, and in certain types of matters, one who specializes in the particular field. There are lawyers who work on nothing but plagiarism, divorce, real estate, negligence, patents, murder or music. There are also a great many general practitioners who handle anything and do it very well.

You are in a better position to choose a good lawyer than almost any other type of professional man, because in selecting a doctor, for example, you can only ask around until a friend says, "Durwurd, if you're looking for a *real* doctor, look no further; I'll send you over to my man; he's the tops. You know me, I wouldn't use any but the best. This fellow — well, *doctors* come to him for advice; you don't want anything better than that!" Or a relative comes out of the ether raving about the magic of Dr. Byfocle or whomever. And you follow the same pattern when you need a dentist or an accountant.

The trouble is, you can't see any of these practitioners in action until they start working on your kidneys, your molars or your books, and then it may be too late for you to care.

But in selecting a lawyer, you have an opportunity to stroll into any courtroom and observe him in the trial of an actual case, and if you like the way he works you can retain him for yourself. He will probably have a card on him.

Here is a courtroom just down the street. Let's go in.

We're in luck. Here is a case where the testimony has just been concluded and the lawyer is getting ready to sum up.

The best case can be lost and the worst case won by the lawyer's summation. It is here that the skill of the lawyer is revealed. Here the lawyer takes the various parts of the case as given piecemeal by the witnesses and weaves them, if he can, into a pattern that will appeal to the jury, and help the jury believe his client.

It is true that many brilliant summations have failed to win cases. This happens when the case itself is so weak that nothing in the world will help it. But, given any kind of a break on the facts, a good summation will pull a case through which might otherwise have been lost.

A lawyer must be a practical psychologist, an actor (a *good* one), a fluent speaker (not too glib), a logician and a gentleman, on summation, if at no other time.

If his witnesses have been weak, he must make them look stronger on summation; if they have been too strong, he must weaken them a little; if their stories have jibed too well, he must explain that.

After he has taken care of these matters, he must do the same thing for his opponent's witnesses, in reverse. This is not a job of work for an amateur. It takes a good lawyer to make a good summation.

Here he comes. He has just finished whispering to that young man sitting at the long table with his head in his hands. The young man is the defendant in a criminal case and the charge is murder. Sh-h-h . . .

Ladies and gentlemen of the jury: You are asked to send this young man to the electric chair — a reasonable demand on the part of the District Attorney; a reasonable demand if you see the facts as he does.

114

But if there is a divine power that guides us all, you won't. I am not going to ask you to "look at my client," in the traditional lawyer's way. I am not going to ask you whether he "looks like the kind of a boy who could commit a murder," because that would be nonsense. Any kind of a boy can commit a murder; and, in fact, my client is not a boy. He is a full-grown man. Besides, as he sits there, with his life hanging in the balance of your judgment, he is in no condition to present a proper picture to a jury. He is overwrought; he is in deepest despair; guilty or innocent, he is a mess. Not because of his guilt or innocence, but because his life is hanging by a thread.

So what is the use of looking at him? That won't help us.

I seek no sympathy for this man. If he murdered Mary Jane he should pay for his crime. It is a crime not only against every decent impulse in a man, it is a crime against God; it is a crime against the State. The District Attorney is right when he refers to it as a "ghoulish act." It is worse. It is worse than any adjectives of mine could possibly make it.

But that is not the point. The point is whether you are going to make my client the victim of a chain of circumstantial evidence as deadly in its way as the lethal weapon that killed this poor girl.

The District Attorney has made much of my client's "criminal" record. He has harped on this man's two arrests to such a point that, were this not a frightfully serious matter, we might have found it most amusing.

Let us see what these two arrests mean. This man was arrested at the age of fourteen for stealing apples! Stealing apples at the age of fourteen! At the age of twenty he was loaded into a patrol wagon for shooting dice in an alley!

115

What a pity that we must be so serious about two such trifling episodes! What a pity that we may not have a chuckle here!

But we must remain deadly serious about those two arrests! We must consider them closely, for they help us to solve this tragic affair! They help us because the *District Attorney didn't bring them out! This man volunteered them!* He furnished this damaging information of his own accord. I do not know whether the defendant is familiar enough with the law to know that a man cannot be asked whether he has ever been arrested; that he may only be asked whether he has been *convicted* of a crime.

But whether he knows it or not, he told us about it himself — it wasn't pumped out of him.

Is such an act the act of a man who is hiding something? Is it the act of a man who trifles with the truth?

Or is it the act of an innocent man, who is helping us find the truth in this case, come what may?

Why, even if he had concealed those two youthful episodes I would not have blamed him. A human being on trial for his life might well reflect that such unfortunate facts, trivial though they were, irrelevant though they were, might put his life in danger. I would not blame him. Nor do I necessarily admire him for revealing them. I think it was a stupid thing to do. I might not have done it, had I been he.

But the point is that he spoke of those things himself! And I think it argues vehemently in his behalf that he is a truthful person.

I believe this man. I should not be able to call forth these words in his defense if I did not. I know my limitations. These words are not mine; they come from a greater power than I possess . . .

116

Might be well to get that man's card; you never know when you'll go berserk and . . . But here's another courtroom. Just listen to these objections! Why do lawyers object so much? No one has yet been able to find out. The fact that he has a *right* to do it doesn't necessarily mean he ought to do it. A witness might be testifying to many things that are objectionable, but which are quite harmless. What is the sense of punctuating that witness's testimony with unnecessary objections? *This* lawyer is really busy:

Q: Tell us about it.

A: Well, there I was. Now, I am an old man and —

COUNSEL: I object, Your Honor. The fact that this witness is an old man has nothing to do with this case!

THE COURT: You are quite right, Counselor. Mr. Witness, you must not say you are an old man.

THE WITNESS: No? Well, what am I, a young man? I am eighty.

COUNSEL: Oh, I object to that, Your Honor.

THE COURT: Object to what, sir?

COUNSEL: I object to the witness arguing with the Court.

THE COURT: Sustained. The witness will not argue.

Q: Continue, please. You were telling us about your meeting with Boozar.

A: Oh, yes. Well, we shook hands. We have known each other for forty years and —

COUNSEL: I object.

THE COURT: Why?

COUNSEL: The answer is not responsive to the question.

THE COURT: You are right. Objection sustained.

Q: Continue, please.

A: Oh. We shook hands, and I couldn't get over his sunburn because —

117

COUNSEL: Object! I object, Your Honor.

THE COURT: You object to the sunburn?

COUNSEL: No, Your Honor. I object to the fact that this witness couldn't get over it. We do not care about his inability to get over the sunburn.

THE COURT: We don't, at that. Try to get over the sunburn as quickly as possible, Mr. Witness.

COUNSEL: Objection! I object to that, Your Honor. Respectfully object!

THE COURT: What now?

COUNSEL: I object to that, too. Your Honor. Respectfully.

THE COURT: A plain objection will do, sir. What is it you object to?

COUNSEL: I object to Your Honor's telling the witness to get over the sunburn as quickly as possible.

THE COURT: You do?

COUNSEL: Yes, sir.

THE COURT: Why?

COUNSEL: Because — I say this respectfully, sir, most respectfully — because it is facetious, and I have a duty to protect the rights of my client and —

THE COURT: You are right, Counselor. I will withdraw my suggestion to the witness. I will also sustain your third objection — or was it the fifth? I have lost track.

COUNSEL: The fourth, sir, the fourth. That was the one where —

THE COURT: Yes, the fourth. That objection is sustained. Let us proceed with the case, please.

Q: You were telling us about your meeting with Boozar, sir. Continue, please.

A: Continue? I can't get *started* . . .

Now, the attorney had a perfect right to make those objections, every one of them, but why should he? What

118

harm if the witness says he is an old man? Everybody in the courtroom can see that. So that objection is useless.

What harm if the witness "argues" with the Court? The judge can take care of himself. So that objection is useless.

What harm if the witness says he has known Boozar for forty years? Why, it might even help *Boozar!* The jury might think he must be a pretty nice fellow to keep a friend for forty years. So that objection is useless.

What harm to mention the sunburn? It doesn't affect the case. So that objection is useless.

What harm if the judge brightens the tedious proceedings with a touch of subtle humor? If the lawyer were alert he would smile with the others and perhaps win the jury over to his side. So that is a useless objection.

Sometimes an objection is worse than useless; it is dangerous. Wait, the lawyer for the other side is getting ready to sum up:

Members of the jury: This case looks mighty suspicious to me. What are they hiding here? What is the defendant afraid of? The defendant hems and haws for two whole days on that witness stand, and we can't get a thing out of him; then on top of that my learned friend keeps objecting to everything. Why does he object so much? What is he trying to hide? He must be hiding *something!* He looks like an experienced practitioner to me. He must know what he is doing.
The minute we begin to get a bit of truth out of a witness, what do we hear? "Object! I object!" Why? Is there something they don't want us to hear about?
He is objecting for a *reason,* ladies and gentlemen! He is *hiding* something!
Don't let him tell you when he comes to sum up that he

119

is protecting his client's interests. I am trying to do the same for *my* client, but you didn't hear any unnecessary objections from me.

Don't let him tell you he doesn't want to "encumber the record" because if ever counsel encumbered a record *he* did, with these constant objections.

No. He is *hiding* something, folks. What is he *hiding?*

THE GRUELING CROSS-EXAMINATION

SOME LAWYERS will cross-examine anybody about anything. The *grueling cross-examination* is very popular in legal circles. Some of the younger members of the bar believe it is the only kind of cross-examination there is. They are like the prize fighter who, at the sound of a bell anywhere, immediately begins to shadowbox. Some of these lawyers, upon hearing the words, "Your witness," immediately rise to their feet and begin the *grueling cross-examination* — which is often a slight mistake.

Let's see:

Every case simmers down to one or two points, some-

120

times three. An ordinary accident case involves these things:

Whose fault was it?

What was the damage?

Let us say that in such a case a witness is called who surprises even his own side by saying, "Well, I really didn't see the accident."

So the lawyer who has called him says, disgustedly, "Your witness."

Whereupon the Younger Member of the Bar rises slowly, clutching a sheaf of papers in either hand, and begins the *grueling cross-examination*.

He inquires into the witness' marital status, his age, his employment, his family background, his relations with the plaintiff; he wants to know whether the witness has been paid for testifying, whether he expects to be paid, whether he is getting a cut from the possible proceeds of the lawsuit, whether he has ever been convicted of a crime; he wants to find out if the witness has ever testified in a case before; if so, how many times and where; also when. He wants to know what the witness was doing on the scene anyway, and is he sure of the date; if so, how is he sure and on what does he base it; he wants to know whether the witness is color-blind or can he distinguish a red light from a green light, and in fact, were there any lights on that corner to begin with.

He may take three hours inquiring into these things, over the protests and objections of counsel, and despite the suggestions of the Court.

And all he should have said was: "No questions."

And then on summation he could say: "Certainly I had no questions to ask that witness. He didn't see the accident."

The lad could go further. He could even say: "I wonder why the other side called that witness anyway. He didn't see anything; he admits it. The whole thing looks mighty suspicious to me."

If this procedure were merely useless, it wouldn't be so bad. It would merely bore the jury and they might get over it. But there is a real danger to useless questioning of a witness. There is the danger of plugging up holes left by the other side in its examination.

We will say that Lawyer Jones calls a witness and, in the heat of the trial, forgets to ask certain vital questions and thus fails to bring out certain information.

Lawyer Brown, on the other side, would certainly do well to leave those points alone. Instead, he asks the very questions himself, or prolongs his cross-examination of the witness to such an extent that Lawyer Jones, sitting silently at the counsel table, has had an opportunity to become aware of the omissions and make the corrections when his turn comes again.

This does not mean that lawyers who are gentlemen want to win cases on points overlooked by their opponents. On the contrary, a lawyer who is also a gentleman will often call his opponent's attention to an oversight and give him an opportunity to make the correction, for he wants to win the case on its merits, and if his side is wrong, he will accept the verdict.

However, there is no point in bringing out gratuitously things that are favorable to the other side.

For example, suppose a lady is suing the railroad company and her lawyer has forgotten to ask her how many children she has.

Now, it is not important for anybody to know how many children this lady has. It has nothing whatever to do with the case.

122

But let us watch the lawyer on cross-examination make a mistake:

Q: By the way, madam, how many children have you?
A: Twelve.

He has done it.

The jury is going to sympathize with a lady who has twelve children. They are not supposed to, but they will. Any lady with twelve children is going to get some consideration. She will certainly get more of it than a lady with no children.

Why did the lawyer make the mistake?

Because he wanted to get in a grueling cross-examination and he stuck that question in while trying to think up a good question. It was a filler.

And it filled him with regret when the case was over.

Another example of helping out the other side:

A man is on trial for burglary. His lawyer has just sat down and the District Attorney has started the grueling cross-examination:

Q: By the way, Mr. Defendant, what is that button you are wearing in your coat lapel?
A: Oh, that!
Q: Yes, oh that, and please answer my questions.
A: Veterans of Foreign Wars.
Q: Foreign wars, eh? Didn't find it somewhere, did you?
A: No, sir. I served twenty-three months overseas.

The District Attorney has done it. But he isn't satisfied. He is going to make it as grueling as possible:

Q: Quite a hero, aren't you! You should have gotten a medal.
A: I did. Two of them. Congressional Medal of Honor and the D. S. C.

Not only has the District Attorney done it, but he has given his opponent a chance to ask a few of *these* on re-direct examination:

Q: Were you wounded while serving your country in the Far East, Mr. Defendant?
A: Yes, sir. A piece of shrapnel got me in the left leg.
Q: Forgot to duck, eh?
A: I guess so.
Q: Is that why you limp a little, sir?
A: Yes.
Q: You didn't get that limp running away from a holdup, did you, sir?
A: No, sir.

Let's follow this thing right down to the summation and see *all* the damage caused by that useless question of the District Attorney's — the filler. The defendant's lawyer is summing up:

Members of the jury: The next time I hear someone ask, "How low can you get?" I am going to have an answer: "As low as a district attorney!" I hope I never become so eager to win a case that I have to resort to what I have seen here today! Not content with dragging every bit of this unfortunate defendant's life in the mud, not content with pelting him with innuendoes, he sees that the jig is up, that he has no case against my client,

and so he attempts to dirty up this patriotic citizen's
very service to his country!

I do not believe, I cannot believe, that you intelligent
and patriotic people are going to be misled by this
moldy device.

If anyone is to be punished here, I have a candidate for
you — and it is not my client!

I thank you.

Yes, the District Attorney certainly did it, and his
chances for governor are pretty slim.

THE JUROR

A GREAT many people, including experts on the subject,
say that our jury system leaves much to be desired, and
there is no question about it, if we go by some of the
verdicts they bring in.

The reason for this state of affairs will be evident if
we look into a few things about it.

To begin with, you are entitled to a trial by a *jury of
your peers,* which as everybody in your set knows means
your *equals.* The theory behind this, one supposes, was
quite sound: twelve men, selected at random from all
walks of life, all adults, could certainly be expected to
understand any kind of a proposition and render justice
with it.

BUT—

SUPPOSE YOU are an accountant by profession — a certified
public accountant, and you have been retained by the

125

Amalgamated Corporation on the eve of their merger with the Consolidated Corporation, to adjust the book value of the preferred stockholders' secondary rights on a pro-rata basis to allow for any equalization residuals outstanding at the time.

You put in a hell of a lot of time and energy on this project, spending the first three weeks trying to understand it, and five months to complete it, at the end of which time you hand over the two-thousand-page report to the president of Amalgamated, with the bill for your fee, $75,000. The president keeps the report, but throws the bill back in your face. He says it is ridiculous. He says $5,000, take it or leave it.

You sue. Amalgamated's defense is that you aren't certified because you went to a cheap school, and the report is wrong, and they have a counterclaim for $100,000 because they had to get a new report.

Now you are in court and your lawyer is selecting a

jury. After two full days of hemming and hawing, challenging, discarding and accepting, the jury is sworn, and your fate is in their hands. This is your jury — taken right from the files:

John Mack, truck driver.
Max Myopa, tailor.
Bruno Metropolous, proprietor of roadside diner.
Elmen Brandish, violinist.
Jennifer Meak, housewife.
Samuel Sparks, electrician.
Alfino Croocut, barber
Emily Yaketté, housewife.
David Drayne, plumber
Mildred Gumm, dressmaker
Langdon Brush, artist
Gloria Dawn, photographer's model

This is your jury, and they are listening intently as your lawyer makes the opening statement:

Members of the jury: . . . and so it is our claim that these secondary rights did not call for *any* equalization residuals, either on a pro-rata basis or on a share-for-share primary basis, which would make my client's two-thousand-page report perfectly correct, as you will see presently, when you will have the opportunity to examine the figures page by page. And now before I conclude, I will ask you to pay particular attention to the column under the heading of Referrals, A and C — you can skip B, because we are making no claim for that. I thank you.

Now the other lawyer:

Ladies and gentlemen: I will merely say this: You *can't* skip B, since this is the very crux of our case, unless you want to leave out three entire columns on page 345 — and I do not believe you will want to do that. I thank you.

Now, this is the jury of your peers and they are going to follow your case carefully and understand every word of it — perhaps not right away, but certainly after the Judge's charge:

Ladies and gentlemen of the jury: It now becomes the duty of the Court to charge you with respect to the law governing this action. You will decide these issues by a fair preponderance of the evidence, which is to say, the greater weight of the evidence. If you find that the plaintiff has sustained the burden of proof you will then examine the extent to which your verdict will apply to the section of the matter which deals with the pecuniary aspects of the lawsuit.

You are not to be swayed by bias or prejudice for or against either of the parties and it will be your exclusive concern to dispense true and equal justice as between these litigants and fairly and impartially appraise the merits of their respective contentions.

You have been here three weeks now, not counting the time lost by reason of the collapse of three of your number, and you have had the benefit of the clear and lucid explanations of these experts in accounting practice, who have drawn the issues sharp and clear and who have given you the sum of their professional skill and knowledge.

It is for you to judge and evaluate the sprawling tentacles of the problem and decide the matter solely upon the equities, without fear or favor —

Now, if we assume that these peers have understood the three weeks of expert testimony, they will certainly understand this charge and you actually need not worry, or it may be that they didn't understand a word of the testimony but dig the charge fine and it clears the whole thing up for them.

However, it is possible that in the jury room this is going on:

JUROR MACK: Does anyone know what the hell this is all about?

JUROR DRAYNE: It's about an accountant.

JUROR BRUSH: Now we're getting somewhere.

JUROR DAWN: Oh, I don't know. If I could remember all those definitions it wouldn't be so hard.

129

JUROR CROOCUT: What definitions?

JUROR DAWN: Oh, you know, the subsideraries and all.

JUROR SPARKS: Me too. Them are the ones got me.

JUROR BRANDISH: I don't say this case is simple, but it seems to me it merely involves a bill for services. The man has a right to be paid or he hasn't. Now, we saw the report —

JUROR SPARKS: Wait now —

JUROR MACK: You stay out of this a minute, mister. Here is an educated man — wears glasses and all; he must know somethin'. What was that again, sir?

JUROR BRANDISH: As I say, we saw the report and, after all, two thousand pages are a lot of pages. I wouldn't want to play two thousand pages of music, I can tell you. In fact, I remember a time —

JUROR SPARKS: But they claim the report was wrong. If it was a wrong report, do you think he ought to get paid?

JUROR YAKETTÉ: Well, really! He ought to get *something*.

JUROR SPARKS: Not if it was a wrong report! What good is a wrong report?

JUROR MACK: Not so fast, buddy. How do *you* know it was a wrong report?

JUROR BRANDISH: He didn't say it was. He said —

JUROR MACK: You stay out of this — sir, I mean. How does *he* know?

JUROR SPARKS: I didn't say it was. I said *if*.

JUROR MACK: Oh, fine.

JUROR MEAK: What about the $100,000 the *company* wants?

JUROR MACK: Take it easy, lady; we'll get to that. Let's stick to this report. How many of you say it was a wrong report?

JUROR DRAYNE: I didn't understand some parts —

130

JUROR MACK: What parts?

JUROR DRAYNE: Look, friend, don't *you* cross-examine *me*. I don't have to tell *you* what parts.

JUROR METROPOLOUS: No heat now, men. What do you say we toss for it?

JUROR SPARKS: Now we're gettin' someplace . . .

This jury could come back in a lot less time than was estimated, and surprise everyone.

But getting back to the jury system — as many astute legal scholars have pointed out, although it has a great many glaring weaknesses, it is the only thing we have to decide questions of fact, and we will have to go along with these peers till we can do better.

IF YOU ARE A JUROR

SOME DAY you may serve on a jury. Before selecting you, the attorneys will ask you certain questions. They want to be sure you will give the parties a fair trial, and their questions are designed to see about that. Right up to the moment of rejecting or accepting you, they will treat you like royalty, because they do not dare let you serve on their jury with the slightest lingering doubt that they think the world of you.

Here, from the files, is the examination of a prospective juror, referred to in legal circles as the *voir dire:*

Q: Mr. Groap, you are listed here as a musician. May I ask with what organization you play?

A: The Tootlers, sir.

Q: Good for you! Member of the union, I take it.

A: Yes, sir.

131

Q: Local 802, eh?

A: Yes, sir.

Q: Great group. Good men. Now, sir, do you know any of the parties to this action? This gentleman here is my client, Mr. Swett, and that tall man over there is Mr. Stoney, president of the Careen Cab Corporation, the defendant. Do you know either of these gentlemen?

A: No, sir.

Q: Do you know me, or my learned friend, Mr. Breakem, who sits there?

A: No, sir.

Q: Now, sir, have you any prejudice against a man who sues for personal injuries; who sues a corporation for personal injuries? I mean, merely because he brings a lawsuit, you do not think any the less of him, do you?

A: Of course not.

132

Q: Have you ever been a defendant in a case; have you ever been sued?

A: No.

Q: Have any members of your family ever been sued?

A: No, sir.

Q: Now, sir, if my client proves to your satisfaction by a fair preponderance of the evidence that he was severely injured and suffered excruciating pain as a result of the negligence of this defendant, or one of its employees, would you hesitate to compensate him adequately for his injuries?

A: Of course not.

Q: You would not hesitate to bring in the full amount of our claim if you thought my client was entitled to that sum, would you?

A: No, sir.

Q: You would not say, "Well, let's give him *something*," and compromise on a smaller sum? You would stand by your convictions, come what may?

A: Yes, sir.

Q: Naturally, sir. We lawyers have to ask these questions, you know; our job. Now, my client is unemployed at the moment, and he has been unemployed for the past nine years. You would not hold that against him, would you?

A: Nine years?

Q: Yes, sir; his mother had some money, but that ran out and — well, you wouldn't hold that against him, would you, sir?

A: Of course not.

Q: You would not sympathize with this — this corporation, would you, this taxicab corporation, or the driver thereof, who, we allege, turned a corner on one wheel at seventy-two miles an hour?

A: No sympathy; no, sir.

Q: Naturally. And we don't want any sympathy for my client just because he suffered this excruciating pain at the hands of this corporation. Now, can you think of any reason at all, sir, why you could not give my client and this corporation a fair and impartial trial on the facts in this case?

A: No reason.

These questions were asked by the plaintiff's lawyer. Now comes the turn of the lawyer for the defendant, and he will go over the same ground, but take a different route.

Q: 802, eh? My old union. Now, sir, have *you* ever been a plaintiff in a lawsuit? Have you ever sued anyone?

A: Yes, sir.

Q: You have?

A: Yes, sir.

Q: Tell us about it, if you will.

A: Well, a truck ran me down over on the West Side; came along like a maniac and couldn't stop in time.

Q: Did that case come to trial, sir?

A: Yes, sir.

Q: May I ask the result of that trial?

A: I lost.

Q: What a pity!

A: Who am I, with an outfit like that!

Q: Exactly, sir. Well, do you think that unfortunate incident has left an impression that would affect your judgment in this case?

A: Of course not.

Q: You could give each of these parties a fair trial?

A: Yes, sir.

134

Q: The fact that my client is not an individual, but a corporation, a small corporation by the way, that would not prejudice you against my client, would it?

A: No, sir.

Q: You could treat the parties as "A" and "B," with an open mind?

A: Sure.

Q: If you came to the conclusion that this plaintiff was a fraud, you would not hesitate to throw his case out?

A: No, sir.

Q: You wouldn't throw him a few dollars out of sympathy?

A: No sympathy.

Most examinations on the *voir dire* run about like that.

The prospective juror who has just been examined would probably not be accepted for service. He would be excused by the defendant's attorney because of that little episode with the truck. The lawyer figures that a man who has himself been a plaintiff will lean toward the plaintiff in the case on trial, especially if the juror has lost his own case.

This is a very popular bit of reasoning among attorneys, but open to question. A very famous railroad lawyer long ago had this matter figured out pretty well. He reasoned that a juror who has been a plaintiff will see through the exaggerations and whoppers of a plaintiff on the witness stand more readily than one without such experience, and he kept such jurors in the box. The validity of his theory is evident when his record of legal victories is examined. He won most of them.

A juror is not supposed to know any of the parties to the case, any of the lawyers, any of the facts.

This was not always so. In the old days, especially in the smaller towns, where everyone knows everyone else, the jurors knew both parties, both lawyers, the judge, the bailiff, and all their families. As for the facts in the case, the jurors knew the facts better than anyone in the room.

Sometimes a juror becomes ill during the trial of a case. If the case is an ordinary, routine trial, the attorneys may agree to proceed with eleven jurors, though this is not done quite as often as it was, since the law was changed to permit five-sixths verdicts. Formerly, the jurors had to agree unanimously. Now, five sixths of their number may agree, and five sixths of eleven jurors make fractions. In a case where the attorneys agree to proceed with eleven jurors, they also agree to accept a ten-to-one verdict.

So that if a juror drops into a coal-hole on his way back from lunch, the case may still go ahead.

In an important criminal case, where the testimony may take weeks or months to be heard, where innumerable documents and exhibits are placed in evidence and experts called, there are two extra jurors, called alternate jurors.

In these important trials, fourteen jurors are selected. They listen to the evidence right up to the end of the case. If none of the jurors has become ill or dropped dead, the two alternates may go home and the case is decided by the twelve main jurors.

When a juror becomes ill and the attorneys do not consent to proceed with a lesser number, the court will declare a mistrial and set the case down for a new trial, at which time it is heard by a new jury.

If the judge should become ill, the case will be adjourned until he is able to sit again. If his illness is protracted, a mistrial will be declared.

If a witness becomes ill, the case is adjourned. If his

testimony is important to the case and he is still ill, a mistrial is had.

Most people are reluctant to serve on a jury and take immediate steps to be excused, on one ground or another. This is tough on people who are waiting for a trial, and it goes without saying that one day the shoe may be on the other foot. Besides, in a shortage of jurors the judge

can always invoke his power to send a bailiff down to the street to collar the first passing citizen and bring him up bodily to exercise his rights of citizenship, and this has been done more than once.

YOU MAY RETIRE

THE FACES of the jurors are very interesting when they are listening to the judge's charge, because he is telling

137

them about the law as it applies to the facts they have just heard, and they are trying to understand the charge.

Some of these charges are pretty deep and the reason is that most of the charges are stereotyped affairs, couched in dry, polysyllabic legal phrases, verbose, redundant, repetitive and so involved that by the time the juror gets a fraction of the first sentence figured out, he is enmeshed in the phrases that follow, and before long he is adrift in a boundless ocean, with words, words everywhere and not a spot to think.

These jury charges are probably handed down from judge to judge, with spaces left for names, dates and figures. A new judge hates to monkey with tradition and reads the appropriate charge for the case at hand, and that is why a juror who is a plumber, a cab driver or a bellhop will be listening to this:

THE COURT: Members of the jury: It is the function of the Court to instruct you as to the law governing the issues herein. There must be no deviation from your solemn oaths to render true and exact justice between the litigants, whether individual or corporate; indeed, to pierce the corporate veil if need be, to locate the crux of the equities . . .

Now, the plumber may get all this without any trouble, as plumbers are notorious for taking their time, on or off duty, but the cab driver and the bellhop are more the nervous, energetic type and may very well miss some of it.

Once in a while a judge comes along and puts it this way:

THE COURT: Ladies and gentlemen, somebody is lying in this case, and it will be your job to find the liar. They

138

can't both be right. Now, you've been here two weeks listening to all these doctors and if you haven't heard enough about this backache you never will. You'll get nothing more about it from me. Now go up to the jury room, figure this thing out, and come back and tell us who gets the money.

Although this charge is written under Poetic License [No. 9132], it could be documented, practically word for word, from the actual files, and there is hardly a juror who would not welcome such a charge.

This state of affairs may furnish a clue to some of the weird verdicts that come back from the jury room.

You lock twelve people in a room after one of these formal charges and then listen at the door. You won't hear any one of them admit they didn't understand every word of it (something to do with the libido). But they're sent up there to have a discussion. And they do — but not necessarily about the case, because they don't dare bring up the subject. But there are many things to talk about — baseball, hats, television — and it is surprising, but eventually a verdict results and the job is done.

Only recently a very serious case was tried and the jury retired. It involved an amputated leg, referred to in legal circles as a "leg-off" case.

The plaintiff demanded twenty-five thousand dollars. The injury was conceded and the entire issue hinged on liability (extent of defendant's negligence), both attorneys hammering away at this intricate question for several days.

So at last the jury got the case and filed out to deliberate. They were gone for seven hours and the waiting was spine-tingling.

At length the judge ascended the bench and sent for the lawyers. He read from a note.

"Gentlemen," he said, "the jury has sent the Court a note. I will read it. 'The jury would like to know if they can give the plaintiff more than twenty-five thousand dollars, or do they have to give him only twenty-five thousand dollars.' "

A court officer fanned the defendant's lawyer back to consciousness, and the judge said, "Of course, gentlemen, I will have to tell the jury that twenty-five thousand dollars is the limit in this case; that they cannot give more." And this reply was sent to the jury room.

The defendant's lawyer was in very bad shape at this point as he whispered to an assistant, "Twenty-five grand! And we could have settled for ten!"

But two minutes after the judge's reply had gone up, down came the jury and announced they were ready to report. Some of the audience even began filing out, not wishing to be caught in the crush only to hear a formality. Then the foreman arose.

"How do you find?" asked the clerk.

"We find for the defendant," replied the foreman.

The judge glared long and hard at the jury, but abandoned whatever he had in mind and discharged them.

No one is permitted to question a jury as to how it arrived at a verdict, but someone buttonholed one of these and got the inside. It seemed that at the sixth hour of deliberation the jury stood eleven to one for the defendant; eleven jurors were of the opinion that no liability had been established, and though the plaintiff had suffered the loss of a leg, they could not, in good conscience, compensate him.

The twelfth juror was stubborn. All he could think of was that amputated leg. He wanted to pay the plaintiff, give him something, at least his medical bill and loss of wages, five thousand.

At this point two of the jurors in a corner of the room became involved in a purely abstract proposition. One contended that a man could not recover more than he sued for; the other said this was not so, that a jury could give him any amount.

This extraneous discussion developed into a heated argument and soon spread all over the jury room, even to the twelfth juror.

It was the twelfth juror who finally settled it. He said, "Tell you what I'll do. I agree with this man here, I think a jury can give any amount. But we'll ask the judge; he ought to know. And if the judge says I'm wrong, I'll swing over and cast my vote for the defendant!"

And so it was. They sent the note down, got their reply, and settled their argument. Whereupon the twelfth juror, as good as his word, cast his vote, enabling the jury to render true and exact justice between the parties.

THE SETTLERS

THERE IS A crucial moment in nearly every trial — civil or criminal. This is the moment when an opportunity arises to settle the case.

If you are suing for $100,000 they might offer $12,000. Should you take it? Or you are being sued for $100,000 and they are willing to take $15,000. Should you give it? Or you are on trial for first degree murder, complete with death penalty, and the District Attorney offers you second degree for a plea of guilty. Should you change your plea or gamble on an acquittal?

Your lawyer will of course advise you, the judge may help with a word or two, your friends and relatives will give their counsel — but the last word must come from you.

141

It is often an enormously difficult decision to make, but with the proper attitude and a little cold-blooded analysis, it can be made a lot easier.

There is an oft-quoted saying among members of the legal profession: "A bad settlement is better than a good lawsuit."

This would seem to be so.

The best-looking lawsuits in the world have been lost at the trial, and the worst-looking cases have been won. If this is so, and we shall see that it is, there is a gamble in every case, just as there is with about every human activity. One cannot even be sure one will cross the street safely.

If this were borne in mind no one would come into court so cocksure of winning his case that he would not be willing to at least discuss settlement. Yet there are such people in the courts every day.

Let us take an ordinary, run-of-the-mill accident case and see if we can settle it.

BROWN VS. SMITH

JOHN BROWN is suing Henry Smith. He claims that Smith, driving an automobile, ran him down as he attempted to cross the street. A simple case.

Brown's injuries, according to his claim, are cuts, bruises, lacerations, and a sacroiliac sprain. His special damages are: two weeks' loss of time from work, a ten-dollar doctor's bill, two dollars for medicines. And his pain and suffering.

Brown wants three thousand dollars — so he says in his papers — but he is willing to take less if the jury says

142

that he must. He hopes they will not make it too much less.

Smith's defense is that Brown appeared suddenly in front of his automobile from behind a parked car and didn't look where he was going. Smith claims he, therefore, doesn't owe Brown a quarter.

Despite this defense, Smith has offered to settle the case for fifty dollars.

Let us not jump to conclusions. We must not think any the less of Smith's defense because he has offered to settle, because the law says that a man has a right to buy his peace if he wishes to do so, and that is what Smith is trying to do; he doesn't want to waste a day or two in court, hire a lawyer, incur sundry other expenses and annoyance. So he has offered fifty dollars.

Brown is indignant! He is dumfounded! Fifty dollars for the cuts, bruises, lacerations, the sacroiliac sprain, the two weeks' loss of wages, the medical bill, the medicines and the pain and suffering! It is preposterous; it is criminal! It is not enough.

Brown wants a trial. He wants a jury to decide this case. All right, Brown, but can't we talk this over informally? Good.

PULL UP A CHAIR, BROWN

To BEGIN WITH, you are not a prepossessing fellow. Now, don't get excited. You have a heart of gold, but your face is against you; you can't help that. Now, how do you testify? Do you tell a clean, straightforward story, or do you stutter and explode, back and fill, and change things around? How is your memory? Are you good at distances

143

and automobile speeds? You weren't drunk that night, but do you take a drink now and then? The lawyer may want to know. What were you doing out at that hour, anyway?

You're sure you crossed at the intersection, now, because that will be important. You may not win if you didn't. But are you going to say you *always* cross at an intersection? That will be a mistake because if you do, they will think you are a liar. Nobody does. But if you did this time, say so.

You're going to remember all this now, aren't you, because we don't want any slip-up on the witness stand. Those lawyers are alert and persistent.

By the way, how is it you remember the date, and the exact time? Was there a parked car on that street at all? *Think* now, because if you say there wasn't, that is going to sound highly unusual; there are usually a dozen on that street all the time.

But if you say there was, don't forget Smith's claim, that you came from behind a parked car. Are you going to put a car on that street? *Of course* you're going to tell the truth! Don't get excited.

Now, these cuts, bruises and lacerations, what are you going to tell the lawyer about those? You're not going to deny that you got hundreds of them when you were young and laughed them off! If you do, the jury won't believe you.

As to the sacroiliac sprain, did you ever hear a lawyer talk about one of those things to a jury? Well, you just catch one of these summations down at the courthouse. He can make it sound almost funny.

About your witnesses now. Are they working? How do they look? How do they talk?

144

By the way, how good is your lawyer? He makes a lot of objections? Well, what's good about that? Sometimes it's better not to object. Does he sum up well? Is he quick to see through a shaky story? How's his memory?

Do you get the point, Brown? Do you see that you're gambling? What's that! You *didn't* cross at the intersection? You crossed in the middle of the block! Why, that's bad, Brown. It may not necessarily make you lose, but it isn't going to do you any good.

Do you see the gamble?

Now, Smith wants to give you fifty dollars. You wait here while we talk to Smith. He may come up a little.

SIT HERE, SMITH

LOOK HERE, Mr. Smith, we know you're not to blame here, but how is your story going to stand up in court? You know how some jurors feel about motorists!

By the way, that "parked-car" defense has been heard in the courts before. It's nothing new. Bear in mind those cuts, bruises and lacerations, and don't overlook that sacroiliac sprain. Did you ever hear a lawyer talk about one of those things to a jury? Well, you just catch one of those summations down at the courthouse. He can make a sacroiliac sprain sound bad. It's even hard to spell. And wait till the doctor explains it on the witness stand!

Do you see what you're monkeying with, Smith? Do you want to take your chances with that jury? They may feel pretty generous today. It isn't their money, you know.

Now, Brown wants a fortune; you're offering peanuts. Make it a hundred and he may take it. Seventy-five? Well, we'll ask him.

145

OH, BROWN

WHAT DO you say, Brown? He offers seventy-five. You'll split the difference? Well, really! —

OH, SMITH

EIGHTY-SEVEN-FIFTY, Smith, what about it? Remember that sacroiliac sprain. Eighty-five flat? Brown won't like this.

OH, BROWN

EIGHTY-FIVE, Brown; he won't budge. You'll take it? Good. You boys have made a good deal here.

It is safe to say that had Brown insisted on a trial and won, the jury would have given him a hundred and fifty or two hundred dollars — and the chances are even that he would have lost . . . a toss-up. But he did the sensible thing, because if the jury gave him more, Smith might appeal and drag the thing along for a year — and possibly win out in the end.

It is really quite simple, basically: you take all the pros and cons of a given situation, weigh them one against the other — all of them — consider the imponderables, the type of judge, the caliber of the lawyers, the appearance of the jury, the state of the weather, the value of your time, and so on, and a decision will present itself.

A criminal case is no different, fundamentally, on the question of whether to settle. If you've got a clean record, good witnesses, a sound defense, a real judge, a good lawyer and a little nerve, you might want to take your chances with the jury, if they are not impossible looking.

If, on the other hand, you are well known at some of the better penal hotels, your witnesses are on the shady side, your defense is for the birds, the judge is prison-minded, your lawyer wears trifocals and you are congenitally nervous, you might want to settle for a short stretch in the can — especially if the jury looks like the first two rows of a PTA meeting.

WHEN YOU TESTIFY

Q: So you're the eyewitness!

A: I was on the corner —

Q: So you're the eyewitness!

A: Why shouldn't I be a witness? Is it a crime? If a man sees a thing —

Q: If you will just listen, please. I asked you whether you are the eyewitness. *Yes* or *no* will do.

A: Yes or no what?

Q: Don't you hear well, sir?

A: What is this? Certainly I hear.

Q: Then why don't you answer the question, sir?

A: What question? What is this? One of us is —

Q: I am sure of it. Are you the eyewitness?

A: What am I sitting here for? Do you think I am enjoying myself? If a man sees a thing —

Q: Yes or no, sir.
A: Yes or no *what,* for Pete's sake!
Q: Are you the eyewitness?
A: *Yes.* Are you satisfied?
Q: Quite. Thank you, sir.

What this witness actually meant was *Yes.* Now the lawyer says on summation:

Members of the jury: Now let us talk about Mr. Finster, the so-called eyewitness. Did you notice his attitude from the moment he took the stand? Did you notice the chip on his shoulder? Now, ladies and gentlemen, I say an unbiased eyewitness doesn't come into court with a chip on his shoulder! I will leave it to you to say what this chip was doing there. How did it get there? Who put it there? I say examine this man's entire testimony, and let the chips fall where they may! But about this particular chip —

Now the whole case seems to be revolving around some sort of a chip on Finster's shoulder, whereas the poor man was simply inattentive and much too talkative. But his carelessness could have far-reaching consequences. If this lawyer didn't have much of a case, and very little to talk about, Finster was playing right into his hands with all this hemming and hawing, for now, instead of talking about the case, he can talk about Finster and this chip on the shoulder, which may look like a two-by-four when the jury finally gets around to deliberating.

Whether you are lying or telling the truth, the surest way to be a good witness is to answer the question directly. If you do that, the most skillful lawyer — or judge, for

149

that matter — is helpless to upset you and will leave you alone in a hurry. Like this:

Q: Now, Mr. Steelmore — by the way, that is your real name?
A: Real name, sir. Steelmore.
Q: You want us to believe you saw the whole thing?
A: The whole thing.
Q: You want to sit up there and tell these intelligent jurors that it was light enough that night for you to see clearly the faces of all these defendants?
A: Yes, indeed.
Q: Do you realize you are under oath, Mr. Steelmore?
A: Oh, yes.
Q: Do you know the penalty for perjury in this state, sir?
A: Can't say for sure. Severe, I suppose.
Q: You suppose!
A: I suppose.
Q: Mr. Steelmore, do you have twenty-twenty vision?
A: I don't know.
Q: You *don't know!*
A: No. I don't even know what it is —

Now, this lawyer is getting nowhere, on the run. His best bet is to get rid of Steelmore. Drop him. Get him out of the courtroom, if possible. And leave him alone on summation. He cannot even be put down as a smart aleck with funny answers. His answers were short, to the point, and responsive, and anything droll occurred in a natural manner. This witness is poison to anyone who tries to break him down.

There is an opposite type of witness who could be called the obnoxious type. He is the joker, who tries to make a fool of the lawyer, with funny remarks:

150

Q: Now, Mr. Witness, your first conversation with this lady was on the 27th. It *was* the 27th?

A: All day.

Q: You seem to recall every detail.

A: I got a photographic memory.

Q: Do you know the penalty for perjury?

A: *You* tell *me; you're* the lawyer.

Q: Mr. Witness, do you find this case amusing?

A: Not very. I wouldn't buy a ticket to it. Not from a broker anyway —

This witness is fairly obnoxious by now, but a good lawyer will give him a little more air time, to make sure. He will conduct his questioning with quiet dignity, ignore all the jokes, with a faint wince. The contrast will put the jury in a mood to strangle this witness with their bare hands.

OOPS!

A WITNESS who volunteers little odds and ends is asking for trouble and there is a good quotation for him to learn by heart: "Ask and it shall be given to you." Such a witness testifies like this:

Q: Madam, to sum it up, this was a rather severe accident?

A: A *rather* severe! It was the worst I ever had.

Q: Oh? Then you have had others! Tell us about them —

This lady may have ruined her case with that little slip of the tongue, because she has opened the door to a grilling about possible previous accidents and the lawyer has a right to show that she sues at the drop of a hat and

151

that this is just another one of her lawsuits, that she is an old hand at it and perhaps her entire testimony should be re-examined. So she would have been a lot better off to have answered "Yes" and called it a day. If just "Yes" cramped her style she could have said "Yes, indeed."

THE MOST

THERE IS another witness who exaggerates everything — but everything. Like this:

Q: Mr. Strech, do you mean to tell us that you remember every word of this conversation?

A: Every word.

Q: A fifteen-minute conversation!

A: Eighteen minutes.

Q: Why, at an average of 150 words per minute that would be 2700 words. You remember every word?

A: Every word.

Q: Getting back to the injuries for a moment, the plaintiff was hurt pretty badly?

A: He was practically killed.

Q: He was bleeding?

A: From every pore.

Q: Come now, not from every pore! Surely that's just an expression —

A: From every single pore. I was there and I saw it.

Q: What about the car —

A: Wrecked.

Q: Well, you mean the front end, the left front —

A: I mean the whole car. A complete wreck. I know a wreck when I see one. This car was wrecked. There was no car.

152

Q: Well, surely some of the parts —
A: No parts, no car. A wreck.
Q: Why, Mr. Strech, you heard these other witnesses say that right after the accident this car was driven —
A: All lies.
Q: Eleven witnesses?
A: All of them . . .

If this witness were just wasting everyone's time it would be bad enough, but he is spoiling what is perhaps a just and reasonable lawsuit because he simply cannot help exaggerating.

BLACK TO WIN IN THIRTEEN MOVES

THERE ARE many absolutely truthful witnesses who make a very bad impression because they try to outguess the lawyer; that is, they try to analyze the question, see what is at the bottom of it, and what it is really leading up to. Now, no one can actually outguess a lawyer, except perhaps another lawyer, and then not always, as we shall see. Take this witness:

Q: Mr. Groap, do you always take three cups of coffee before going to bed?
(Groap — to himself: Now, what the hell is *that* all about!)
A: Do I always what?
Q: Do you always take three cups of coffee before going to bed?
(Groap — to himself: Maybe he thinks — no, can't be that.)
A: Three cups?
Q: Three cups of coffee — before going to bed.

(Groap — to himself: Could be that he knows — ridiculous; I never told a soul.)

A: Before going to bed?

Q: Before. Do you?

(Groap — to himself: This man is driving me crazy! Why
don't the judge make a ruling or something!)

A: What is the question? I don't get that question.

Groap doesn't know it, but the lawyer doesn't want
him to *get* that question — he just wants him to answer it,
because he is laying a foundation for a certain point about
nineteen questions later. Groap will never figure this out,
but he will succeed in looking like a very evasive and
shifty witness, with his constant echoing of questions and
parts of questions, and even though the jurors don't understand the question either, they will begin to wonder why
Groap doesn't answer it and suspect that perhaps he is
hiding something.

THE TIGHT SHOES

SOMETIMES THE shoe is on the other foot, and it is several
sizes too small: there are times when the *lawyer* tries to
outguess the *witness:*

Q: Doctor, you have testified at great length here about
the properties and characteristics of polystyrene as dis-
tinguished from this new material known as dylon, and
speaking for myself at least, your testimony has been
most impressive. *But,* Doctor, the sphere of polystyrene
is thermal engineering, whereas the sphere of dylon is
chemical engineering, is that not correct?

A: That is quite so.

Q: Now, you have a degree in chemical engineering.

A: Yes; I testified to that.

Q: *But you do not have a degree in thermal engineering!*
(The witness polished his glasses carefully and in a gentle, fatherly tone gave his answer.)

A: I should be loath to challenge the integrity of the faculty of Oxford University, which conferred upon me the honorary degree of Doctor of Thermal Engineering, sir.

So that you *can* play games with lawyers in a courtroom if you are a Doctor of Thermal Engineering and are not afraid to speak up.

If you are not a doctor and cannot pronounce polystyrene, about the only thing left is this:

Q: Mr. Witness, I have been very patient with you, but I must insist on an answer to the question.

A: Well —

Q: Really, sir, I don't think you'll find the answer on the ceiling, which you have been inspecting so carefully. You are taking up the time —

A: Let's see now —

Q: It isn't on the walls either, Mr. Witness — Your Honor, this witness is plainly stalling. I ask the Court to direct him to answer the question forthwith.

THE WITNESS: Your Honor! He had three years to think up the question. He won't give me three minutes to think up an answer!

It is like going into battle: if you're sure the gun is loaded, you may fire.

155

YES OR NO

NOTHING PUZZLES a witness more than those three words.
The lawyers, the judge, the court officers, even the porter
in the hall, seem to be screaming at him to "Answer
yes or *no.*"

And the worst of it is that he must — unless he can't,
and thereby hangs a new paragraph.

In the old days it was the custom to allow a witness
to tell his story in narrative form, and it came out something like this:

Q: Now sir, you have said that your name is Dither and
   that you live at the edge of the mall, in the house with
   the green door. Tell us what you know about this
   affair.
A: Well, Your Worship, it was about three by the dial,
   and this particular sundial was accurate because it
   was given me by my great-uncle, who was a stickler
   for accuracy. Indeed his name was Stickler, which was
   probably the reason for his obsession — or perhaps
   'twas the other way around. In any case, I was afoot
   upon this day, my horse having been taken with the
   plague, and I was not at all enjoying the hot, dusty
   road, I can tell you, sir. Of a sudden, out of nowhere,
   so it seemed, came this madman, astride a beast fully
   as mad, upon my oath, and charged me, as if I had
   drawn my sword — which I had not, and which
   indeed I could not have, since I had gone abroad
   without it, due to my miserable wyfe's inattention to
   her duties. I have not decided what I will do with this
   wretched woman. She lies abed of late until six of the
   morning, and no matter how often I beat her, at which
   I assure you I am not remiss, her tongue is never still

— fagh! it rings in my ears even now — when she re- moves my boots at eventide there is no gentleness in her; when she scrubs the floors it is with awkward, noisy movement, so that a man cannot enjoy his pipe. But her latest inpertinence will do her in — and this I swear — she mutters about wanting to eat her supper at my table and balks at walking behind me when I am abroad — this is upon my oath! In any case, I was without my sword and feeling naked, I assure you. Drafty anyway —

Well, with an answer like that the jury might wind up with a verdict for the horse. The answer was so full of ex- traneous material, it was difficult to follow, and it violated a great many rules of law, so the narrative form was gradually dropped, and the question-and-answer system adopted. The theory was all right, because a lawyer was an expert on the rules of law and could so streamline his question that all that was left for the witness to do was say *yes* or *no*. This was supposed to be a terrific time-saver because it would eliminate all references to wives and great-uncles and sundials and the like, and speed things up.

But it hasn't worked out that way because often the lawyer streamlines the question so thoroughly that the witness doesn't understand it, and it must be repeated or restreamlined, so now it takes a lot more time than it did before. However, they are working on it and it may come out all right in the end.

That is why you must answer *yes* or *no*.

PARADOX

THERE IS A curious thing about this *yes* or *no*: The lawyer insists on it, and yet there are times when such an answer infuriates him. This is when he is asking you certain trick questions which are supposed to make you angry, or make you sputter, stutter and explode, or so upset you that you don't know what you're talking about. In such a case, even though he is *insisting* that you answer *yes* or *no,* he is *expecting* that you will do no such thing, and when you cross him up and give him a yes or a no, you aren't playing the game. Take the old chestnut:

Q: Do you still beat your wife?

A: No. (So far so good, *but:*)

Q: Oho! So you admit you have beaten her!

A: Beat who? Listen here! Why, I never beat my wife. I never hit a woman! The only time —

Q: What was that?

A: Nothing.

Q: "The only time — " you began to say.

A: What only time?

Q: Finish your answer.

A: I finished my answer.

Q: You said "The only time — " What *was* that? Just what *was* that, sir?

A: Wait a minute — that's not beating —

Q: What's not beating, sir?

A: Is a *shove* beating?

Q: You shoved her? When did you shove her? Give us the date. The date of the shoving, please. Your Honor, we want to know about the shoving!

THE COURT: We certainly do. Give him the date.

THE WITNESS: Gosh, I didn't write it down.

Q: You shoved her, but you didn't write it down!

A: Well, no. Would *you* write it down if you shoved her?

Q: Indeed I wouldn't. Well, let's see if we can't help you

158

with the date. Perhaps these hospital records will give a clue. Your wife has been in and out of several hospitals?

A: Well, yes; four children —

Q: But here are five hospital visits. What about that fifth hospital visit?

A: Oh, that was the stairs.

Q: What stairs?

A: The whole flight.

Q: You threw her down a flight of stairs?

A: I did not! All I did —

Q: Continue.

THE WITNESS: Your Honor, is this a federal case?

THE COURT: Not yet. Now answer the question.

A: What question?

Q: All you did was what?

A: All I did was shove her.

Q: And the flight of stairs?

A: That was her own idea . . .

Now, if this witness had just kept his head and answered *yes* or *no,* no one would have known about the shoving or the stairs. (He actually *did* throw her down the whole flight; and it wasn't a shove, it was a left hook to the jaw — always effective.) But the lawyer knew that if he got the witness mad enough he would spill something — and he did.

See how different this same deal is, when properly done:

Q: Do you still beat your wife?

A: No.

Q: So you admit you have beaten her?

159

A: No.

Q: Didn't you just say, etc.

A: No.

IF IT CAN'T BE DONE

SOME QUESTIONS cannot be answered *yes* or *no,* in which case it is no disgrace to say, "I cannot answer that *yes* or *no."*

The curious thing is that many people would rather plead guilty to murder than to ignorance, and the words "I cannot," to many, have the ring of ignorance, so they give the oddest answers to these questions:

Q: You knew that if you stepped on the brake you would not stop in time, so you stepped on the gas, even though the plaintiff stood there in the roadway, in your full view, with a porcelain vase in either hand, a magazine tucked under one elbow and a dog's leash gripped tightly under the other — with a dog at the other end?

A: I refuse to answer that question.

Q: You *what!*

All hell breaks loose here, because this kind of talk from a witness is strictly out of bounds, not cricket, and against the rules. The pity of it is that the witness doesn't mean that at all. He simply means: the question is so involved I don't understand it, and if I did I don't believe a *yes* or *no* would cover all the points — but he is ashamed to confess all this and be thought slow-witted. This makes him a little angry, so he can't think straight; therefore the answer — which opens the floodgates; which adds confusion to confusion and has him practically knocking at the prison doors:

Q: You *what!*
A: I will not answer that question.
THE COURT: I have an idea that you will, sir!
THE WITNESS: But, Your Honor —
THE COURT: You are not running this court, sir!
THE WITNESS: I don't *want* to run the court, Judge —
THE COURT: Then answer the question.
THE WITNESS: But the question is so —
THE COURT: Do you need a hearing aid, sir? I didn't say *analyze* the question; I said *answer* the question! . . .

By the time the smoke clears away the witness looks like an international spy, and all this need never have happened.

DO YOU WANT US TO UNDERSTAND . . . ?

A LAWYER CAN put six little words in front of a perfectly proper and innocent question and make you give an answer you might not otherwise dream of uttering.

Q: *Do you want us to understand* that you remember all these dates!
A: Well, come to think of it, I guess not.

There is a magic ring about those six words that throws a witness off, makes him unsure. There are variations, with the same results.

161

Q: *Do you want this jury to believe* that you saw Grew-som on the 29th?

A: What do you mean do I want them to believe?

Q: *Do you want this court to understand* that you never saw Dreggs in your life?

A: To understand? Who understands? Everybody knows that Dreggs and I — that is, me and Dreggs never — what was the question?

Q: *Do you want these intelligent jurors to believe* you are sure about the date?

A: I never said anybody was not intelligent. All I said was that if the date — I already gave you the date.

Q: *Do you want* to change your answer?

A: What answer? I didn't change any answer.

Q: Do you read and write English?

A: Do I read and write English! What kind of a question is that? Who doesn't read and write English? What am I, a Communist?

Q: Were you ever convicted of a crime?

THE WITNESS: Pardon me, Judge, is he allowed to accuse a man? I am a witness, Judge. I am telling the truth here —

The idea is to get the witness flustered, angry. An angry witness doesn't think clearly. A witness who doesn't think clearly is a sitting duck in a shooting gallery.

This doesn't mean that lawyers spend all their time making witnesses angry. They reserve this technique for the witness with whom they are getting nowhere. Say a witness is lying beautifully. All day and into the late afternoon he murmurs quiet, logical answers to the questions and is getting away with it in great shape. The lawyer is weary with frustration. He knows the witness is lying, but cannot seem to blast him out of it.

162

Well, a few Do-you-wants may do it — and often do.

THE PARTING-SHOT QUESTION

THIS IS A beauty, and it works nearly every time. When the lawyer has apparently finished with you, he will sit down — then immediately get up and ask the Parting-Shot Question or Quickie. Here is such a question, answered by an intelligent witness:

Q: You are friendly with the plaintiff, aren't you?
A: Yes.
Q: You want to see him win this lawsuit, don't you?
A: Yes.
Q: Has he promised you anything out of it?
A: No.
Q: Are you sure?
A: Quite.

Here is the same question, answered by a sitting duck:

Q: You are friendly with the plaintiff, aren't you?
A: Who, me?
Q: You want to see him win this lawsuit, don't you?
A: Well, if a man — take anybody that has ever had — What was the question?
Q: Has he promised you anything out of it?
A: Well, look here — now, Judge, this man, this counselor, has no right — I don't take a thing from anybody.
Q: Are you sure?
A: Is who sure? Look here now —

If this witness gets mad enough — and he will — something will slip out about a date or a secret meeting or a piece of change, and he will be knee-deep in this:

Q: All right; now we know there were three fifty-dollar bills? What about those bills? Give us the dates!
A: I gave you the dates — two dates. I don't remember the third date. But the fourth time —
Q: Oh, there was a fourth time!
A: Well, the way you keep shouting — Your Honor, could I have a glass of water? . . .

THE BY-THE-WAY QUESTION

LOOK OUT for this one. This is worse than the Parting Shot. It is pure dynamite. A question that starts with "by the way" will catch you off your guard if you are not paying the strictest attention, and you may find yourself on the wrong end of this:

Q: By the way, Harry, you didn't kill Dripp, did you?
A: *Who didn't? I certainly did!*

You let a thing like that slip out and they may want to know all about it.

This By-the way question is a fascinating thing to watch, when properly done. The lawyer says, "That is all, sir," and takes his seat at the counsel table. He looks away from you as though he wants nothing further from you. He taps a pencil lazily on the table as though waiting for the next witness. Then, carelessly, with a half-turn, as if the question meant absolutely nothing at all, just an afterthought, he murmurs:

Q: By the way, what did you do with the body?

164

That by-the-way part is so soothing, so disarming, you not only wind up telling them, but you may warm to the subject and tell about other bodies as well.

SO YOU DON'T TALK!

A SURE-FIRE method of making a witness look bad is based on the fact that witnesses hate to admit they have discussed the case with anyone. Some witnesses would rather go to the gas chamber than admit such a thing. The question has an ominous implication and the witness has a feeling it must be wrong to have discussed the case. So:

Q: Have you discussed this case with anyone?
A: Who, me?
Q: You, sir.
A: Why, of course not.
Q: Surely you don't mean that!
A: I certainly do. Now, look here —
Q: You never talked to a soul about it?
A: Not a soul.
Q: Well, let's see now. You are married?
A: Of course.
Q: Did you ever discuss this case with your wife?
A: No, sir.
Q: Mr. Fetherhedd, are you really listening to my questions?
A: Of course I am.
Q: You saw this attractive woman on the sidewalk, brandishing the umbrella like a weapon, screaming unmentionable words at the man who turned out later to be her husband, you saw her lunge forward to gouge out his eyes with it, you saw him duck, and finally you saw the umbrella jammed tight into the mouth of this

165

passing policeman. You observed his astonishment at the whole thing, you helped to extricate the umbrella, and you were in the patrol wagon helping to pry the woman loose from the husband. In fact, when they couldn't get her to stop scratching him up, you were the one who suggested filing her nails, and did it on the spot.

A: That's right.

Q: But when you got home that evening you didn't discuss it with your wife!

A: No.

Q: By the way, what time *did* you get home that evening?

A: Late. About eight o'clock.

Q: You have told us your wife is very strict about this. What did you tell her?

A: I told her I had a flat tire.

Q: Why?

A: I didn't think she would believe the other thing.

Q: Well, surely she didn't go for the flat tire!

A: No, sir.

Q: And you wound up telling her about this occurrence?

A: Well, I *mentioned* it.

Q: Of course! What did she say?

A: Nothing. What could she say?

Q: Surely she asked you what the woman was wearing?

A: Well, that's a fact. She asked that.

Q: And you told her.

A: Sure.

Q: And she asked about the unmentionable words?

A: That's right; she wanted those.

Q: And you mentioned them?

A: Yes, sir.

Q: All of them?

A: All I could remember. Quite a few there.

Q: When you told her about the fingernails, she asked about the shade of nail polish?

A: How did *you* know that? I mean yes, sir.

Q: And you told her.

A: I didn't know the exact name of the shade. There's over a hundred shades.

Q: But she got this information from you anyway?

A: How did *you* — yes, sir.

Q: She mentioned the shades, one at a time, until you got the right one?

A: Not the whole hundred. I think about the thirtieth question is where I came to the right shade.

Q: And of course your wife wanted to know what finally happened to the woman?

A: Well, yes.

Q: And you told her.

A: Yes, sir.

Q: She showed some interest in the husband too, didn't she?

A: No. What do you mean?

Q: She asked whether he was handsome?

A: Well, that, yes.

Q: And you told her?

A: Yes, sir.

Q: How long did this conversation with your wife take?

A: About two hours.

Q: So that, Mr. Fetherwate, you *did* discuss this case with your wife!

A: Well, if you call that a discussion.

Q: Don't *you* call it a discussion?

A: I don't know what to call it. Can I have a glass of water? . . .

It takes all day, but the lawyer finally brings out that

167

Fetherhedd has discussed the case not only with his wife, but with all the boys at the office, with the traffic cop uptown, with his manicurist, with the bartender at Joe's and with a few other people around the courthouse. Now the jurors are ready to believe absolutely anything the lawyer may care to say about him, and he will say plenty.

A good witness can not only handle this thing right, but he can trap the lawyer, or help the lawyer trap himself:

Q: Have you discussed this case with anyone?

A: Oh, yes.

Q: You have?

A: Certainly.

Q: With whom?

A: Let me see; with my wife, the boys at the office, a traffic cop, a fellow at Joe's and a few other people.

Q: Did they tell you what to say here? Did anybody tell you what to say?

A: No.

Q: Are you sure?

Q: Quite.

Q: Did the lawyer tell you what to say?

A: No.

Q: Are you sure?

A: Yes, sir.

Q: Did he ask you about the facts?

A: Of course.

Q: Did you tell him?

A: Certainly.

Q: What did you tell him?

A: I told him that your clients were definitely on the wrong side of the road at the time of the collision, that they went through the red signal light and committed every violation in the book and that they really ought to be behind bars rather than behind a wheel, and furthermore —

This lawyer made the mistake of asking for a conversation, and he got it.

WHY?

LISTEN FOR this word when you are testifying. It's like getting a free ticket to the ball game. When a lawyer asks "Why?" it might be a big mistake, and permit you to say things you otherwise couldn't. For example, you wouldn't dream of calling a lawyer a jackass in open court, yet if he asked for it:

Q: Mr. Witness, do you think this trial is a joke? Why are you grinning?

You have a perfect right to reply:

A: Because only a jackass would ask the questions you've

169

been asking me all morning, and when I think of a jackass standing up in a courtroom it makes a funny picture, that's why. I saw a picture once —

Now, the lawyer might object all over the place, but he hasn't a leg to stand on, because he merely got an answer to his question. He asked why, and the witness told him.

There was an actual trial, in which a witness was being mercilessly cross-examined. For three hours by the clock the questions poured on. At length the cross-examiner paused for breath and asked the court's indulgence for a moment to look for something among his papers.

During this respite, the harried witness wiped his brow, chewed on a pencil, then suddenly found a small card and made a brief note on the back of it. He was about to put it back into his pocket when the keen-eyed lawyer observed the movement. Up went his arm. "Just a minute!" he shrieked. "What is that paper? Let me have that paper!"

The witness paled.

"I want that paper, please!"

The witness found a handkerchief and mopped his face.

"Your Honor," shouted the lawyer, "will Your Honor direct the witness to produce that paper!"

The witness was panic-stricken. He seemed to be debating a leap through the window. He squirmed and coughed and wiped his face over and over.

The judge leaned toward the witness and said gently, "Give me the paper." He took it from the witness and gravely read it. Then he asked quietly, "Shall I read it to you, Counselor?" and the lawyer triumphantly cried, "If you would, please." And the judge read:

"This man is an idiot."

YOU CAN'T DO THAT!

THERE ARE a great many things a witness is not permitted to do in a courtroom, and for many this is a great hardship. A man goes through life collecting hundreds of handy clichés and learning to use them at the drop of a hat; they become part of his conversation and are as natural as breathing. Suddenly he is compelled to drop them like a hot coal and talk like a scientist or a statistician and it is difficult.

For example, you cannot give hearsay testimony. Here is an answer which is chock-full of hearsay and is therefore worthless, for it will be stricken out by the court:

A: So on my way home I meet these boys from the club and they tell me that Dugan was the one who done it. This is hard for me to believe because I remember what the blond waitress tells me only the day before about him being too smart to get mixed up in a thing like that, so I make up my mind that I will think it over for a while.

This witness would never get beyond the word "Dugan." Counsel would be on his feet with a motion to strike out the answer, and out it would go. *Facts* are the big thing in a courtroom. The place for hearsay is over a beer at Mike's or, if you are a lady, under the dryer at Gaston's.

CONVERSATION

THE SAME thing goes for conversations. If you are testifying against a defendant you cannot tell about a conversation at which the defendant was not present.

Say John Slickery was on trial for swindling. Imagine how he would feel if you were allowed to say this:

A: Now I personally never met Slickery, but this man with the beard came rushing into Mike's that night with fire in his eye, screaming something about a refund. He told me Slickery sold him a money-making machine that didn't work. I said, "Surely you're kidding, friend!" He said, "Am I?" and he opens up this valise and shows me this ridiculous box with the chimney and the trap doors, and about twenty small bottles with colored fluid. He said, "The red juice is for ten-dollar bills, the green for twenties, the blue for fifties — " and I stopped him. I said, "You mean to say you *bought* this?" He said, "I can see you never met this man." I said, "What did you give him for it?" "Twelve thousand dollars!" he screamed. Well, I nearly spilled my beer.

I got him to show me how it worked. He said, "You put the paper the size of a bill in this slot, and through this hole on top you drop the chemical. Then you wait five minutes and watch the chimney. If white smoke comes out, it needs more juice, if black smoke, the money will be finished in sixty seconds."

I said, "What kind of smoke did you get?" He nearly choked. "No goddam smoke at all! It's a fake, is what it is, and I'll kill him!"

This kind of an answer would certainly be unfair to Slickery, especially if he were actually innocent of the charge and didn't sell the man the machine at all, but maybe only the special paper.

The machine and the transaction mentioned here were not a nightmare, but the subject of an actual case in a federal court, in which the defendant pleaded guilty to attempted swindling. This poor man made a double mistake: he was not only caught in the act, but he pleaded guilty before a brand-new judge, who looked down at him benignly and asked him to explain his operation.

The judge's kindly, fatherly attitude was so disarming, the defendant became downright enthusiastic, deftly manipulated the bottles of colored fluid, flapped the trap doors open and shut, slid the blank paper in, pulled out crisp fifties and hundreds until it seemed the judge himself and the first two rows of lawyers were going to buy in, and the little man glowed with pride. It was the legal consensus that morning that the rap would be a year and a day, in view of the fine co-operation of the defendant.

But in the end, the judge said, in a gentle, fatherly tone: "Ten years."

"HE WAS CRAZY AS A LOON."

You CAN'T say that. It is a conclusion. You can say what you saw, but the *jury* must say he is crazy. If you want a jury to believe the man was crazy, you must give the facts:

A: I first met him on the 11th, at a cocktail party given to launch the author of a new book, *Girls Are Fun*. He was in a corner discussing Proust with a man about ninety when this breath-taking redhead nearly fell into his lap, her dress having caught in his vest button. She murmured, "Oh, dear! Would you help me with this thread? I'm afraid I'm stuck." He looked her over coldly and snapped, "Can't you see I'm busy?" The ninety-year-old guy was so shocked at this rudeness he untangled the broad himself and walked away with her. On the second occasion I was on the town with an expense account and two ravishing beauties from the Copa line. I called him on the phone and invited him to make it a foursome. He said he was reading *War and Peace* and wanted to finish it.

Now, if the jury wants to decide from these facts that the man was crazy, they may do so.

"HE WAS GOING VERY FAST."

ANOTHER CONCLUSION, and inadmissible. You must say how fast, in miles per hour, and let the jury decide whether that was very fast. Jurors get paid for doing just that. And you can't say, "He was driving like a maniac," unless you want to start that whole thing with the girls again.

"HE KNEW I WOULD PAY HIM BACK."

How DO YOU know he knew it? You are not a mind reader, you know.

"HE IS A LIAR AND HE KNOWS IT."

THIS IS A double conclusion. Only the jury can call a man a liar. And who can say whether the man knows he is a liar but the man himself? Not even the jury can do that. Sometimes not even the man knows it, and the records are replete with the files of men who lie so automatically they are never sure about anything. (*See* chapter on Marriage and the Good Life.)

174

"HE WAS DRUNK AS A LORD."

ANOTHER DOUBLE conclusion. You cannot say a man was drunk unless you first qualify yourself as an expert. Here are the questions you would be asked in order to qualify:

Q: What is your profession?
A: I am a police officer.
Q: Have you, in your professional capacity, come in contact with people who were charged with intoxication?
A: Yes, sir.
Q: Were any of those persons later found to be intoxicated?
A: Yes.
Q: How many were found to be intoxicated?
A: Hundreds.
Q: Can you recognize the odor of alcohol on a man's breath?
A: Yes, sir.
Q: Did you detect alcohol on this man's breath?
A: Yes, sir.

Now you can say the man was drunk, because it is evident that you know a drunk when you see one.

If you want to indicate that a man was drunk, and you can't qualify as above, there is a way. You may say that he staggered, that he walked unsteadily, that his eyes were glazed, that he mumbled incoherently.

Of course, these symptoms could indicate other things than intoxication, but, again, it is for the jury to say what they indicate.

Even a doctor is sometimes not permitted to make the flat declaration that a man was drunk. True, a doctor is not asked a lot of qualifying questions because his expert-

175

ness is assumed, but he might have to go into a great deal of detail to show how he arrived at the conclusion.

A doctor may give his medical conclusion or opinion, and any expert may give an opinion on a matter within his field, though as we have seen, even such an opinion can be examined to show how it was arrived at.

EXCEPTIONS

ALL OF THIS does not mean that one may never say a man looked sick or tired or whatever. It depends upon the importance to the case of the man's condition. If the matter is not of very great moment, opposing counsel will not bother to object, in the interest of saving time. As with many other matters, if the statement does not materially affect the case, a good lawyer will let it go in.

You may be sure, though, that if the particular proposition means much to the case, you are not going to get away with a conclusion or an opinion.

"MY WIFE TOLD HIM TO FIX IT."

YOU CAN'T say that, unless you were there when she told the landlord to fix the defective stairs or whatever it was, because that would be a conclusion. If your wife told him to fix it, *she* will have to say so.

"IT SEEMED STRANGE . . ."

PERHAPS IT did, but you can't mention it, because what might seem strange to you would seem quite normal to someone else. Remember that fellow with the girls?

176

"I TOLD HER SO MANY TIMES."

No GOOD. You must say *how* many times, and if you can-not be exact, *about* how many. Remember, *facts* are wanted.

"HE BOUGHT THE PROPERTY FOR A SONG."

SHREWD CHAP, but the testimony is no good. How did the tune go — in dollars and cents? We want figures, and if you don't know, say so.

"I ALWAYS TOLD HIM TO BE CAREFUL."

TOO VAGUE. Always is a long time. *When* did you tell him to be careful? Like this:

A: On the night of June 23rd I met him at Mike's and I told him to be careful.
Q: Did you tell him again?
A: Yes. On July 3rd I told him to be careful.
Q: Yes?
A: And on August 8th I told him: "Be careful."
Q: By the way, was he careful?
A: No. Her husband finally found out about it and that's what caused this accident — or whatever it is.

DID YOU GET THE MONEY?

HERE IS A question that panics a lot of witnesses and often ruins their entire testimony: "Are you being paid for coming to court?"

177

Now, let's say you are a plasterer and earning — well, drawing — thirty dollars a day, plus fringe benefits, and you see an accident and become an important witness.

Well, you'd like to come down and testify for the party, but you certainly wouldn't want to lose that thirty a day and those fringe benefits, so the party agrees to pay you for any lost wages, which is fair enough, and perfectly legal and proper.

But witnesses don't know this, and when they hear the question it sounds like an accusation, and they testify like this:

Q: Are you being paid for coming to court?
A: Who, me?
Q: Come to think of it, yes, *you.*
A: Why, no.
Q: *What!*
A: Well, I saw the whole thing and when this man —
Q: Look here, sir, I don't believe my question is complicated. Are you being paid for coming to court?
A: I wouldn't accept money from any man —

About fifteen minutes of this wrangling and finally this answer is pried loose: "Well, yes."

Now the witness looks like a real thief and any explanation to clear it up sounds like an afterthought, so he is actually taking the plaintiff's money under false pretenses, since he has nearly ruined the case.

An informed witness does it like this:

Q: Are you being paid for coming to court?
A: Certainly.
Q: How much are you being paid?
A: I will be reimbursed for any time lost from my work.

178

Q: Nothing more?
A: Nothing more.

This witness is worth not only the thirty a day, but the fringe benefits as well — and may get them.

KEEP AWAKE — CURVES AHEAD

THIS NEXT question is definitely not for sleepy witnesses:

Q: When did you slow down to the legal rate of speed?

See what the lawyer is doing? You never said you had ever gone faster than the legal rate, but the question *implies* it, and if you answer too quickly, you may wish you hadn't.

STOP SIGN

A GOOD PLACE to stop talking is right at the end of a short answer, which is another way of saying don't give the man more than he is asking for, because you may be giving away your case on a silver platter. Here is an actual answer that will live forever (it has already lived half that) : In a collision between a train and an automobile, the plaintiff's lawyer was getting nowhere with the grizzled old-timer, who stuck to his story that the moment he heard the train whistle from afar, he grabbed his lantern, ran to the crossing, and stood there swinging it, right up to the instant of impact. The jury bought the old gateman's story and turned the plaintiff out of court.

179

Later, the yard foreman said, "Zeb, you didn't say whether the lantern was lit." And the old guy said, "Nobody asked me."

ASLEEP AT THE SWITCH

YOU CAN BE switched into an answer you don't mean. Suppose you've been testifying you are sure the thing happened on Fourth Avenue, whereas the lawyer would be happier if you said Third Avenue. Suddenly he says, "Now, Mr. Drousy, tell us on which side of Third Avenue the thing happened."

And sleepily you say, "On the east side, of course."

You can explain your head off later, but the lawyer will have the last word on summation:

Ladies and gentlemen of the jury: A greater man than I said it: The end justifies the means! [He puts it that way because he doesn't know who said it.] It was an heroic measure, but I had to do it. I knew this witness had strayed from the path of truth when he kept talking about Fourth Avenue, and I am sure you knew it too. So we had to get him back on Third Avenue, where he belonged in the first place. Well, when a man is relaxed he will tell the truth — it has something to do with the brain cells. Anyway, at the moment that he was relaxed I put the question, and I did it for *you,* ladies and gentlemen, because I knew you wanted the truth here, and we got it. Now let us analyze the rest of his testimony and see that he lied throughout —

(*See* chapter on Sleep and Your Glands.)

180

THE BOY STOOD ON THE
BURNING DECK

You are looking for trouble if you memorize your story, and the lawyer will help you find it.

It will *sound* memorized — depend on it. But what is worse, after the first rendering, which you may have carried off beautifully, there is the cross-examination. This is where the lawyer takes the story apart, piece by piece, and makes you say it sideways and backwards, whereas when you learned it, you figured on a straight run-through.

Suppose, for example, you have witnessed a serious accident occuring on a ship bound for Europe; seems there was gold aboard, the ship was hijacked in mid-ocean, a terrible battle ensued, with every available man taking part, including the captain's twelve-year-old son.

Well, it's an important case and you don't want any slip-up, so you memorize your story:

The boy stood on the burning deck
Whence all but he had fled;
The flame that lit the battle's wreck
Shone 'round him o'er the dead.

But now comes the grueling, rapid-fire cross-examination:

Q: This boy, now; isn't it a fact that you didn't see this boy at all?

A: Who, me?

Q: You didn't actually see the boy, did you?

A: Why, he stood on the burning deck.

Q: Yes, you have told us that; but there was a lot of excitement at the time, what with the flames and all. Isn't it possible you're just guessing about this boy?

A: Why, whence he had all but fled —

THE COURT: Are you chewing gum, sir?

THE WITNESS: No, Judge.

THE COURT: Speak clearly, please.

Q: The fact is, the deck was deserted, wasn't it?

A: Well, the flame that lit the battle's wreck . . .

THE COURT: The answer is stricken as not responsive. Was there a boy at all, sir?

THE WITNESS: I'm not sure, Judge. Could I have a glass of water?

If the lawyer has done his work well, you are in one of several positions at the end of the cross-examination — none of them good. You may have finished up admitting that the boy wasn't on the deck at all, but had gone below because he was a coward, or that *you* had gone below while *he* was fighting the flames, or that there was no boy, but a few men running away from the battle's wreck, which you couldn't see clearly, due to the smoke from the flames.

On the other hand, if you weathered the cross-examination (unthinkable) and your second version matched your first version, you are in real trouble, because the lawyer has detected a memory job and will take you over the ground a third time.

182

If your third version stands up with the other two, you may as well call your family and set your affairs in order because you are going on a vacation. You see, the lawyer will now ask for a recess, have your entire testimony transcribed, and then in open court all the versions will be compared and found the same. The judge and jury will know you memorized the whole thing.

There is a way to beat this deal: memorize the story three different ways, with plenty of changes in each version, then get a friend to cross-examine you for two hours, and memorize *that*. If you're good at memorizing it can be fun.

HALF NELSON WITH A FULL TWIST

SOMETIMES, the way a lawyer words a question and the way he delivers it, will make you mumble things you didn't intend to. He may look at you severely and say:

Q: You want this jury to believe that you stood there talking to this man for fifteen minutes, yet you can't tell us the *color of his suit!*

A: Well, I've never been in court before —

The way you're reacting to this question, you seem to be on the defensive and you look bad. *This* is the way:

Q: You want this jury to believe that you stood there talking to this man for fifteen minutes, yet you can't tell us the *color of his suit!*

A: Exactly.

Now the *lawyer* looks bad. He seems to stand corrected, as if you had said, "Why, of course, you silly boy!"

183

DANGER – LAWYER AT WORK

YOU MIGHT be a very important witness in a very important case and kill the whole thing if you trip over this one:

The key question that is asked of an eyewitness concerns the manner in which he saw the happening, or how it came about that his eyes were on the spot at that precise instant; for it is often the case that a witness honestly deceives himself into thinking he *saw* it, when in fact he *heard* it first, and looked an instant later. Naturally there is a vast difference.

So you have been testifying for two whole days that the reason you actually saw this thing when it occurred was that you were looking up the road for a taxi and naturally couldn't help seeing the whole thing.

But you're up there on the witness stand, and just as you are about to doze off the lawyer says:

Q: And the crash, you're sure you heard the crash too?
A: Well, of course.
Q: And you're sure it was this crash that first attracted your attention to this occurrence?
A: Naturally.

Now, don't waste your time trying to squirm out of it, because – sh! . . . the lawyer is summing up:

Ladies and gentlemen of the jury: Well, it took us a long time to get to the crux of this thing, didn't it! But we made it, didn't we! *Now* we know exactly what happened here, don't we! And it amounts to this: *he didn't see the thing at all!* He *heard* the *crash,* looked around, and tried to figure out what happened! Well, we will thank him to keep his theories to himself and

184

not try to foist them upon an intelligent jury. This is a democracy —

TRICKS OF THE TRADE

IF YOU TESTIFY very well and come through everything with flying colors you may make an excellent impression upon the jury, but the lawyer will feel hurt and try to think of something to erase this impression or put a dent in it.

There was a case in which an excellent surgeon was testifying. Preceding this surgeon on the stand had been an eminent orthopedic surgeon, who had given a contrary opinion. The general surgeon, however, had made a brilliant impression, and the resourceful lawyer knew it, being a keen student of psychology and its effect on juries. He finally came up with this question:

Q: Doctor, are you an orthopedic specialist?
A: No, sir. I am not.
Q: The fact is that you are just a general surgeon?
A: No, sir! I am not.
Q: You are not? Well then, exactly what are you?
A: I am a general surgeon and not just an orthopedic specialist!

So that, if you are a general surgeon, speak well and have patience; that question will come along and you will be all set.

THE EXPERT

IF YOU ARE an expert in some particular field, it is not

185

desirable to become too technical in your testimony, or this might happen:

Q: Now, sir, you are a machinist and you were in charge of this project?

A: Yes, sir.

Q: Tell us briefly how you got the machine to working properly.

A: Well, there were burrs under the screw heads and the cam arm rotated laterally, with a thrust on a three-to-four ratio. I simply reversed the directional impact, deburred the screw heads, took three thousandths off the inside diameter, put a spindle valve between the breast plate and the pantograph, nursed the split-putter into position, with a diagonal for accuracy, and rammed half a dozen mill ends into the dead center.

Juror No. 3: Well, I be goddamned!

The Court: Mr. Juror, normally I would be inclined to punish you severely for contempt of court, but I will overlook it this once. The fact is, the Court was thinking exactly the same thing!

You get this juror into trouble and you certainly can't expect any favors from *him*.

THE REAL YOU

As you walk toward the witness chair, remember this: the jurors are looking you over, and deciding, before you open your mouth, whether to like or dislike you. It isn't legal, but it is human. So it is only necessary for two or more of this committee to decide you are not their type, and that ends your usefulness before you start.

There are several ways of making a good preliminary impression.

1. Dress as well as you can. This can be overdone, of course, but a well-dressed person commands respect everywhere. Take a fellow in his mid-twenties, charged with mugging, assault and a touch of robbery in the first. He walks toward the stand in a quiet, neatly pressed blue suit, an immaculate white shirt with conservative tie, clean-shaven, hair combed, shoes brightly shined. It simply doesn't make sense to connect this fine-looking young man with all those uncouth activities and, for the moment anyway, he makes a great impression. Of course, if it comes out later that the clothes are stolen and that his finger-prints match the ones found on the victim's head, that is another matter. But that first impression *was* excellent.

2. When you take the oath, look the man straight in the eye, raise your right hand firmly, palm open, and respond in a clear, positive tone. This will show you mean business and are ready for the worst, which may turn out to be a good thing before you are through.

187

3. When you testify, sit back in your chair, comfortably and relaxed. Look straight at the jury and make your answers clearly and distinctly.

4. Don't chew gum. If only three out of the twelve jurors detest gum chewing, it is a safe bet they will also detest gum *chewers,* and you're *it.* There is a further drawback to gum chewing. We have seen there are judges who don't like plaintiffs, others who don't like defendants. Well, there are still others who don't like *witnesses.* Well, such a judge might suddenly snap at you, "Take that gum out of your mouth!" Startled out of your wits, you probe for the gum and find it. But as you sit there with the sticky stuff between your fingers, you feel stupid, with all those people watching as you try to figure out what to do with it. You are about to put it back and swallow it, when the court attendant steps up and hands you a piece of paper. Now the jury and everyone else in the courtroom waits while you wrap it and put the package in your pocket. It is an awkward spot and could very well cost you a few votes.

5. Don't lose your temper; keep calm throughout.

6. Don't keep saying, "Who, me?" or "What was the question?" or "I didn't get that." If you do, the jury will know you are lying. Remember, a lot of these jurors are married men, and they have done a little testifying in their time, under the worst possible conditions, with no rules of evidence to protect them, with no judge to make rulings, and without even court attendants to keep order. They will know the score in a hurry.

7. Don't let your ego get the better of you, like that man in a recent assault case, who kept testifying how peaceful he was, how he wouldn't harm a fly, how he had never laid a hand on a soul. But the lawyer knew different, and began to needle him, and deliberately got his goat

188

with a number of personal and annoying questions, ending up with this:

Q: You're not afraid of my client, are you?
A: Ho! I can murder a roomful of him and not get winded!

Well, the jurors did a character-reading job on this witness and made a few changes in their first impression.

8. Last, but most important: Tell the truth. It is most relaxing. And then, too, you're under oath. Naturally *you* won't be lying, but the trick is to make the truth sound *true*. That's when rules one to seven will help you.

6

THE FINE PRINT

THE FINE PRINT
THE FINE PRINT
THE FINE PRINT

How's YOUR VISION? Do you see spots? Well, it would be better if you stopped fooling with spots and spent a little more time with fine print, though there have been cases where the fine print brought on the spots, or maybe it was the other way around. In any case, the fine print will kill you if you don't watch out. For example:

Are you *really* insured? Easy, now! Remember what the doctor said! But you *do* drive your car around as though you hadn't a thing to worry about, and this could be a mistake.

You carry personal liability insurance, with $10,000–$20,000 limits? That's nice. That's what the average man carries, and it is certainly a comfort to know that if you hurt anybody with your car, the insurance company will defend you free, and foot all bills within the limits of the policy — $10,000–$20,000, and that's a lot of money.

BUT —

THESE LIMITS mean that in a particular accident, if *one* person is injured, the insurance company will pay *up to* $10,000, and if several are injured *in the same accident*, the company will pay a total of $20,000.

Well, take that *one* person. It would be great if he had the decency to confine his injuries to $10,000 worth, but suppose he is very seriously injured — nearly killed — and is entitled to $76,297.23 — which the jury says is very fair. How do you stand? The company pays $10,000 and *you* pay $66,297.23, which is a lot of money even in counterfeit bills.

Not too long ago there was a very serious automobile accident. A car, containing five people, went through the plate-glass window of a big department store.

All five were injured, one very seriously.

Now, the driver of the car carried insurance to the limits of $100,000–$300,000.

The badly injured plaintiff received a verdict of $265,000, the other four, $5,000 each, making a total of $285,000 in damages.

The insurance company paid the full limits of its policy: $100,000 for the *one* person, and $20,000 for the other four, making a total of $120,000 for the entire accident, and the car owner chipped in the rest, $165,000, which, fortunately, he didn't mind, having had a very good week. But he did remark to a friend later that he hadn't thought about his policy quite that way and was going to read it first chance he got. It was his view the company should have paid their $300,000 limit, since the whole business occurred in *one* accident.

191

But the friend pointed out that the policy distinctly read: $100,000 for *one* person and not more than $300,000 for all, as the result of *one* accident.

This car owner is thinking about increasing his policy limits to $500,000–$1,000,000, but for the time being he is driving in second gear.

THE LAME, THE HALT
AND THE STATED

FROM THE standpoint of insurance, it is sometimes a pleasure to be ill. This is when you have a *stated* illness, and if you ever get around to reading your health-and-accident policy you will find that is the only illness that counts, which means that if you get any of the illnesses listed (or *stated*) in the policy, you will be paid.

Some will complain it is a bore to wait for Trichinosis of the Upper Intestine (lower doesn't count) or Accordionist's Bursitis (no other instrument) or Polar Expedition Elbows (South Pole only), but the policy plainly says *stated* illnesses, and leaves no room for ambiguity, if you will only read it.

If and when you ever *do* get any of these things, there will be no quibbling about payment, provided you get them at the times stated in the policy and in the manner stated in the subdivision, which is fair enough, because a policy is a contract and you are supposed to read a contract before you sign it.

THE HOUSE WITH THE GREEN DOOR

THERE WAS a very sad case recently, involving a beautiful house with a green door. The green door has nothing to

192

do with it, except maybe to identify the house, as we shall see.

This house was down at the shore. It was handsomely furnished and solidly built and a great delight to the owner, especially in the summertime, when he could sit of an evening and listen to the soft murmuring of the waves and watch the moon drift lazily among the stars.

As soon as he bought the house this owner lost no time insuring it, because he figured it would be unthinkable to have anything happen to it, and he got the works, including extended coverage, which insured the house against the perils of *windstorm, hail, explosion, riot, riot attending a strike, civil commotion, aircraft, vehicles, smoke, except as hereinafter provided.*

Well, one night this owner had to stay at the office on business, and as he looked out of the window he began to worry about the house, because dark, ugly clouds darkened the sky, the wind whistled furiously, and thunder and lightning blasted the heavens.

He cut his work short and made the last train down to the shore.

Only there was no shore.

A tidal wave had swept the whole area; a windstorm such as no man had ever beheld roared like a mad hurricane and whipped the ocean's water against anything still standing.

And there was no house.

The beautiful house was gone, ripped from its foundations, lashed into a million parts, and as the utterly crushed owner stared out at the angry sea he caught a glimpse of the green door — on its way to Ireland.

Nobody knows how long he stayed there in his sadness, but when the storm subsided and he could think more clearly, he suddenly brightened, and before long he was grinning all over — he remembered his insurance policy, with the extended coverage and the hereinafter provided, and he envisioned his home again, even more beautiful, on the same spot, with palm trees maybe, and a lot more, for the insurance money would take care of it.

And now the sad part. This man knew what he *was* covered for, but he had no idea what he was *not* covered for, because he had not read his policy, he had only signed it, and that is not enough. When he got the policy it said *at the top,* in big, black, capital letters: *Perils of windstorm, hail, explosion, riot, riot attending a strike, civil commotion, aircraft, vehicles, smoke, except as hereinafter provided.*

But those last four words killed him, because the *hereinafter provided* clause, on the same page, said this:

Provisions applicable only to windstorm and hail: This company *shall not be liable* (1) for loss caused directly or indirectly by (a) frost or cold weather, or (b) ice (other than hail) , sleet, snowstorm, waves, tide, tidal wave, high water, overflow of streams or bodies of water, or spray therefrom, all whether driven by wind

194

or not; (2) for loss to the interior of the building (s) or the property covered therein caused by rain, snow, sand or dust, whether driven by wind or not, unless the building (s) covered or containing the property covered shall first sustain an actual damage to roof or walls by the direct force of wind or hail and then shall be liable for loss to the interior of the building (s) or the property covered therein as may be caused by rain, snow, sand, or dust entering the building (s) through openings in the roof or walls made by direct action of wind or hail; or (3) for loss by water from sprinkler equipment or other piping, unless such equipment or piping be damaged as a direct result of wind or hail.

Naturally the company wouldn't pay a quarter, because there was this tidal wave, and under the hereinafter-provided clause they were not liable *unless the building (s) . . . shall first sustain an actual damage to roof or walls by the direct force of wind or hail.* The poor owner couldn't prove this, because he was down at the office, not watching the house. He was very bitter about this at the trial, and the court had to admonish him:

THE WITNESS: Sure I liked my house, but do you mean to say I had to be down there watching it to see about the direct force of the wind, or which came first, the wind or the water! All I know, there was this terrible windstorm, and my policy says windstorm. Besides, even the hereinafter clause says the company will pay if the water entered the building through openings in the roof or walls made by the direct action of the wind —

Q: *Provided* the house is *first* damaged by the *direct* force of the wind. Was it?

195

A: Well, of course it was.

Q: How do you know, sir?

A: How do I know! Didn't you hear about this wind-storm? It was in all the papers. It was the worst wind-storm in the history —

Q: But how do you know, sir, that the *water* didn't do the first damage, and not the *wind?*

A: Well, what made the water do it, if not the wind?

Q: So you admit the water did the first damage!

A: I did not! I said *if* the water — Your Honor, my policy says "windstorm." Even Your Honor knows this was a windstorm —

THE COURT: What is *that!*

THE WITNESS: I mean Your Honor knows —

THE COURT: Watch it, sir!

Well, the poor man finally passed away in the hospital, and nobody knows for sure whether it was from the loss of the house or the loss of the case or the loss of his mind.

Incidentally, his heirs may be in for a surprise, because his life insurance has a suicide clause and if it can be proved that he did the whole thing deliberately, there will be trouble collecting on the policy.

It would certainly seem that it is more important to *read* the policy than to sign it.

WE, THE PEOPLE

INSURANCE IS A great idea. In fact, it would be impossible to live without it, or die without it, for that matter. It is the people who buy it that cause most of the trouble, for in addition to not reading the contract, they buy either the wrong kind of coverage, or not enough of the right kind.

196

To get an idea of how important insurance is, let's say you go into the five-and-dime store and buy a box of matches for a dime. If there were no insurance, you might have to pay fifteen or twenty cents for this box of matches, or give up arson, cooking, smoking, or whatever you bought them for.

Because the manufacturer of the matches insures his product against possible lawsuits by reason of some defect in the product. A customer might use a match and get a splinter — lawsuit — fifty thousand dollars — blood poisoning — pain and suffering — medical bills — loss of earnings (concert violinist, $5,000 per performance).

If there were no such thing as insurance, this manufacturer would have to jack up the price of the matches to take care of these lawsuits, and the expense of defending them.

Apply this to bread, cheese, booze, nylons, pianos and the thousand and one necessities and the picture is clear.

So insurance is definitely here to stay, and it has been so extensively developed that it would be practically impossible to find a legitimate human activity that is not covered.

There is, of course, life insurance, to protect your loved ones after you have worn out your nose on the grindstone.

Endowment insurance, to cover you if you live too long.

Industrial insurance, to bury you.

Fidelity insurance, to watch over your cashier.

Strike insurance, so you can talk back to your help.

Annuities, so you can laugh in your beer.

Title insurance, so you know whether you are fixing your own roof or somebody else's.

197

Automobile insurance, so you will dare take the car out of the garage.

Jewelry and fur floaters so that if your wife is missing you can carry on.

Comprehensive insurance, so you can let come what may.

These are some of the commonplace and generally known forms of insurance, but it is astonishing how many other kinds there are. It would take the entire book to list them all, but here are a few you might want to look into:

Paraphernalia Floater: This covers scheduled flags, banners, uniforms, religious articles and vestments, lodge and other paraphernalia.

Musical Instrument Floater.

Neon signs.

Extra expense policy: Insures against payment of additional expenses while operating in temporary quarters due to damage to building.

Fraternal Protective: Insures against robbery, burglary, larceny, forgery and embezzlement, in case one of the brothers loses his head and makes off with the dues.

Rain Insurance: If it rains.

198

Key-Man Insurance: Say you don't know anything about the business, but your key man does. You lose him and you might have to close up the shop. Your wife won't like that; so this is a good buy.

Depositor's Forgery Bond.

Glass Insurance.

Manufacturer's Special Hazards.

Passenger liability.

Paymaster robbery.

Yacht Policy: Insures yachts used solely for pleasure purposes.

Removal of Debris.

Valuable Papers.

Non-Ownership Explosion. This covers you if you don't own the thing that exploded.

Salesman's Sample Floater: In the case of a piano sales-man, it is easy to see how valuable this insurance is. Some of these pianos are mighty expensive, especially the big grands. You carry one of these around for a while and then have something happen to it, you won't be sorry you have the insurance.

Office Burglary: Many have often wished an office burglar could be covered. Well, he can.

Bridge Insurance Policy: Unfortunately, this is not contract bridge, which has still not been quite worked out; it is an ordinary bridge. But if you have a bridge, it might be wise to cover it.

Earthquake Insurance: Not to be confused with house parties in apartment buildings. This is covered by a different form.

Partnerships: Nothing to do with wives. There is no insurance against wives. But the insurance people are not asleep; the actuaries are kicking it around and may come up with something.

Pharmacist's Malpractice: If you take the wrong poison, it covers the pharmacist. You get covered by a different form.

Outage insurance: Pays an hourly indemnity for each hour or part of an hour that a described object is completely or partially out of use. Very handy.

Demolition Insurance: Nothing to do with children. This is for buildings.

Trees, Shrubs and Plants: Covers direct or indirect damage.

Consequential damage: Nothing to do with philandering. This covers light, power, heat, etc.

Residence and Outside Theft: This is for farmers, on or off the premises.

Fidelity bonds: Nothing to do with husbands. This is for employees who handle money.

Accountant's Liability Policy: This covers an accountant if he makes a mistake in the figures. Very handy for people who are weak in arithmetic.

Lawyer's Insurance: Covers lawyers who forget to cross-examine.

The list of coverages is practically endless, including Apiaries, Artists, Appraisers, Billiard Parlors, Blacksmiths, Blowers, Carpenters, Caretakers, Courthouses, Dog Kennels, Engravers, Fish Packers, Guest Houses, Hat Cleaners, Jails, Lecture Service Agencies, Locksmiths, Museums, Nut Stores, Osteopaths, Pawnshops, Ranches, Screw Machine Products, Tree Surgeons, Upholsterers, Veterans' Groups, Watchmen, Wreckers, Youth Groups.

And there is even *Insurance Company Insurance*, by which an insurance company is insured against loss, like anybody else!

So insurance must be a pretty good thing, if they buy

their own product, and you can bet they read the policy before they sign it.

ONLY . . .

Now, ABOUT reading the policy. It is actually very simple if you know what to look for. We have seen that it is more important to know what you are *not* covered for. But how do you go about finding this out?

Surely nobody's eyes are powerful enough to read *all* the print. But there are certain *key* words to look out for, and you can spot these if you rest your eyes in between the readings. These key words are: Stated, Scheduled, Named, Specified, and Insured Hazards.

Notice that you will rarely, if ever, find the word "only" in the policy. Nobody knows for sure why this is. One theory has been advanced: that the company is afraid the policy will fall into the hands of a child, who could very well understand the word "only," and would go on to read the rest of the policy, which would take up his time and interfere with his school work — but this is only a theory.

So instead of "only," they use these other words, and, paraphrasing the wording, they say:

We hereby insure you for all stated hazards.

Then they state the hazards:

1. Falling off an Alp, 9200 feet high, with gloves on.
2. Lousing up Indian Rope Trick, in room 30′ x 50′.
3. Giving wrong change for $10,000 bill.

201

Well, there is the trouble: The man buying the policy sees the one line on top which says *We insure you for all stated hazards,* and he signs right away. He doesn't read the *hazards,* because he is attracted by the word *all,* which anyone will admit is an attractive word and seems to cover everything.

If a common citizen were writing the policy, it would probably read this way:

This insurance is *only* for a 9200-foot Alp, an Indian Rope Trick and a $10,000 bill, and it must all happen the way we say or you don't get paid.

All this would be right at the top, in big, black letters. Well, it would be easily understood all right, but there would hardly be a customer for such a policy. The prospect would give the agent a hard time. He would say, "Do you think I am out of my mind? Where would I find an Alp, or a $10,000 bill, and what do I know about an Indian Rope Trick, in a room that size?"

But when the agent hands over the Standard Policy and says, "Do you notice, sir, that this covers *all stated hazards?*" the prospect can't wait to get his hands on the pen, for fear the agent will change his mind and refuse to issue the policy.

A *stated* risk is the same as a *scheduled* or *named* or *specified* risk. In fact, all these *key* words mean exactly the same thing, but they sound a lot better than *only,* and are not as monotonous.

It comes to this: even *stated* insurance is better than no insurance, and if you shop around it may very well be that there is a policy which insures against non-insurance.

202

THE RELAPSE

ONE OF THE strangest cases on record, having to do with fine print, occurred on Park Avenue in New York. On a bright, sunny afternoon a man decided to go to the hospital. There was nothing the matter with him, but he had hospitalization and hadn't been getting along too well at home. He decided to stay in the hospital for a week and rest up.

Just before making this decision he had come from the renting office of an apartment building, where he had signed a lease, and he had the lease in his pocket when he entered the hospital.

He asked for a sunny room and began living it up, with pretty nurses coming and going, and good food and so on. But in the evenings, with the nurses gone, and no radio or television handy, he felt like reading.

He hated to ring the bell for the night nurse, who was definitely not in a class with the day nurses. In fact he had worked up a positive dislike for this nurse, and yet he wanted to read.

He glanced idly around the room and suddenly saw this lease sticking out of his coat pocket.

And that is how he came to read his lease.

He settled himself among the pillows, adjusted the reading light, lit a cigar and began to read, and for quite a while he was all right.

But it was a Standard Lease, and eight thousand words, in very, very fine print, and nothing untoward happened for over an hour.

Suddenly this man became violently ill, began ringing

203

all the bells, hurled his shot glass through the window, and nearly set the hospital afire with the cigar.

Well, everybody came on the run and they finally got him under control and lashed firmly to the bed, but all the hospital people agreed it was the worst relapse they had ever seen.

The story finally came out, when the psychiatrists moved in the next day. It seems this man had come to the clause in the lease concerning dogs:

19. No animals of any kind shall be kept or harbored in the demised premises, unless the same in each instance be expressly permitted in writing by the Landlord, and such consent, if given, shall be revocable by the land-lord at any time.

Well, when the man read this clause he blew his top, because he was very fond of dogs and wouldn't be without one. But he knew the landlord would never permit this dog in the house, in writing or otherwise, because the animal was as big as a polo pony, and that even if he did get the consent, by some miracle, it would be revoked by the landlord the minute he laid eyes on this dog, and it would all be legal, under the lease.

Before he knew what he was doing, he was reading the other clauses, one worse than the other.

The shot glass went through the window when he came to the clause about No Television after 11 P.M. (This man was strictly for the Late Late Show.)

The bells began ringing when he saw a clause that No Matter What Employee of the Landlord damaged his property, the Landlord was not responsible.

The cigar got to the pillows when he got to the paragraph about No Singing or Piano Playing at Any Time of the Day or Night.

Hysterically, he croaked to the psychiatrists that it seemed to him that under this lease he could live in the house and pay the rent, provided he sneaked in and out and didn't make a sound. But at the end of his raving he had a lucid moment and said grimly, "We'll see what a jury says about this!"

But the psychiatrist said, "I am afraid you won't! You can't have a jury, according to this lease! Clause 23 distinctly says that you have signed away your right to a trial by jury! Even if you fall nineteen floors down an elevator shaft because of the negligence of the landlord, and break every bone in your body, you have no right to a jury!" The man turned purple.

"But the Constitution! The Constitution of the United States distinctly says —"

The psychiatrist shook his head sadly. "Clause 23 here is stronger than the Constitution, because you signed it. You didn't sign the Constitution."

Well, before they finally let this man out of the hospital, they spent four days reading this lease to him, word for word. They figured if he got to reading it at home he would go into a real-estate coma, which is the worst kind, and might never come out of it.

So they lashed him to the bed real tight and read the whole eight thousand words of fine print, which they had no trouble doing because they have these powerful microscopes for the hospital work.

They read the clause dealing with *Remedies of the Landlord,* which shows what happens if the Tenant doesn't toe the mark; they read about *Waiver of Redemption, Fees and Expenses, No Representations by Landlord.*

They had to give the man a shot of adrenalin with this last one, because it showed that the Landlord makes no promises of any kind and the tenant moves in at his own peril.

They read the clause about *Measure of Damages,* which figured out in advance how much the Tenant owes the Landlord if the Landlord ever decides to sue him.

Then the *Access to Premises* clause, the *End of Term,* the *Inability to Perform.*

They had to give him another shot for the last one, because it explained in advance why the Landlord can't perform his end of the lease and is therefore not to blame, and under no circumstances should the rent stop coming in.

These psychiatrists were lucky they were coming at last to the end of the lease, because the man fainted at the very last part. But they were ready for this, because as they were reading it, one of the psychiatrists fainted. It was the clause marked *Definitions,* which showed that under certain circumstances the *Landlord* might not even be the *Landlord,* in a legal sense.

Well, if this strange case doesn't point up the value of reading your lease, somebody has been wasting a lot of time.

PASSING THROUGH

As you pass through this vale of tears, there are a great many simple things you can do to avoid trouble or a lawsuit, and it is really surprising that people don't give a thought to them.

Say you owe a man forty-seven dollars. You've been putting him off for some time and at last you find yourself able to pay. Now, this man is a good friend, but it is well

206

known that he hasn't a good memory. Yet you certainly don't want to ask him for a receipt; he didn't ask you for one. Well, you can pay him and *make* him remember. Like this:

Hand him forty-seven *one*-dollar bills. Simple as that. Can't you see yourself saying later, "Why, Joe! How can you say I didn't pay! Don't you remember I handed over forty-seven one-dollar bills? And you punched me right in the mouth! Why, here's the scar, Joe!

If you've actually got a scar, that wraps it up, of course. But even without it, Joe will remember, because the whole thing is so unusual.

AT THE REGISTER

A MAN GOES into a store, buys something and hands the cashier a twenty-dollar bill.

Now, many cashiers put this bill on the top or on the ledge of the register, in plain sight, while they make change, to avoid disputes.

But some don't.

So the next time you hand a cashier a twenty-dollar bill, you say in a loud, clear voice, before he puts his dirty hands on it: "Twenty dollars." Then, if he doesn't make the right change you're in a much stronger position, because everybody in the store will have heard you say "twenty dollars," and he won't have a leg to stand on.

Of course, you'll run into this: Some cashiers are sarcastic, due to handling all this money for the greedy owner, and such a cashier might say, "I see it, mister; I'm not blind!" To which you can reply, "I want you to hear it too, pal; I'm not bashful!"

If this doesn't do it, there is always a punch on the nose.

207

THE SHORT CUT

IF YOU ARE among the many who like short cuts, an excellent short cut to trouble is the *deposit*.

Say that you're a short, stout man, standing about five-two on tiptoes and you pass a store window showing a handsome worsted overcoat with a colossal fur collar, modeled by a man of distinction. The minute you behold this coat you know it was made for you and you enter the store.

You try it on in front of the mirror and are stunned by the beauty of the coat, and you turn this way and that as you ask the price. The salesman is also stunned, but he keeps a straight face and asks whether he should send it or will you wear it.

Suddenly, as you are about to answer, you think of your wife. You weigh everything she has ever said to you about your size, your general appearance, your ridiculous taste in clothes — and your confidence begins to ebb.

But the beauty of this coat is overpowering. The tired old brain goes into action and comes up with the answer: put a deposit on the coat, then go home and have it out like a man.

So you hand over fifty dollars, get your deposit receipt, shake hands with the salesman and leave, taking a last, proud look at the coat.

THE GATHERING STORM

BACK AT THE apartment, things are not going too well. Your wife says, "You will get a coat with a fur collar over my dead body."

208

And you give her the one that was good enough for your father and his father before him: "That might be arranged."

But, like your father and his father, you win all the battles, but you lose the war, and you are immediately back at the store, waving your deposit slip and demanding your money.

You are stunned again. You can't get your money, because you have bought a coat. There it is, right on the slip: One coat, $195. On account, $50. Balance, $145.

Suicide is out of the question: you would be the first in the family and disgrace the name. Flight? Impractical: you have tried to hide from her before, but she has Royal Canadian Mounted blood, on her mother's side.

So you pay for the coat and give it to a friend and have the vicarious pleasure of at least seeing it every day.

So the trick about a deposit is to make sure it is actually a deposit, and the way to do that is to have the man write on the slip, "This deposit is returnable on demand," or any other short phrase that will make it clear that you get your money back without question.

If any store refuses to do this, you want no part of it, or the coat. Often a salesman will say, "Oh, don't worry about a thing, sir. If you're not pleased, or if you change your mind, bring it back for a refund."

But after you leave, the boss, who may have overheard this remark, fires the salesman, and you look stupid when you come back for the refund. Even if the salesman is still working there, he may say that you misunderstood; that he was joking; that they never refund; that you may have a coat with a bigger fur collar if you like, but the refund is out.

Buying a house or renting an apartment involves the same thing.

You might be apartment hunting on a beautiful Sunday with your wife. You see the Very Thing and decide to take it, but even though she has fallen in love with it, you know this is by no means final, as it will take thirty minutes to get home, and this is ample time for her to *detest* it. So you put down a deposit and the man gives you a receipt.

You get home, take off your coat, hang up your cane and tackle the Sunday papers. Suddenly she says, "You know . . . I've . . . been . . . thinking —"

Without a word, you put the paper down, take your coat and cane, get the car out of the garage and are off to get your deposit back.

You may be amazed to find:

1. You can't get your deposit back.

2. You have signed a three-year lease, and your rent begins at once.

The reason is this: If a receipt contains the principal elements of a lease, such as the apartment number, the rental, the term and date of occupancy, and that this first payment was on account, it is fully as binding and legal as a lease, and the full, eight-thousand-word lease merely explains in detail why you can't do this, that or the other thing, when you can come and go, and so on.

Divorce is no solution to this problem, because in most states this is no ground for divorce.

These few illustrations can be distilled into one basic thought: *any* time you sign a paper of *any* kind, be sure it says what you want it to say, and do not be bamboozled by a remark that it is.a "standard" form, or a "standard" receipt, or a "standard" whatnot. Just tell the regal proprietor you want to add a word or two so you'll both be happy. If he refuses, it is a good indication that he doesn't

210

want to be happy and you're better off without him *or* his goods.

A prominent lawyer has been having trouble with his own wife about this from the day they were married. She has no confidence in herself and every time she buys something she is not sure. For twenty years she has been saying to this lawyer when he comes home from the office, "Would you do me a favor, dear?" and he always says, "Where did you buy it, what did you pay for it, where is the receipt and why do you want to return it?"

He blows his top every time he looks at the receipt, because she never remembers to have the store add that she can get the money back, so he must go to these different stores and argue, cajole and threaten. Very often he does all right and brings back the money, but he is often missing a tooth, or a necktie, or his face is cut. It is hard work.

The stores are puzzled about this woman. The lawyer never says he is her husband — he is ashamed — but he does mention that he is a lawyer, and they think she hires a lawyer by the year just to return these dresses, stockings and bras. They wonder how she can afford it. But the husband wonders, too, so it is about even.

211

7

HOW IT ENDS

WHY NOT watch an entire case from beginning to end and see what happens?

BANG!

We're off. That bang up there is the crash of two automobiles making contact.

A crowd gathers. More people now, coming from everywhere.

The driver of one of the cars creeps out of his vehicle, pale and badly shaken up. His name is Henry Brown. His car is the Plymouth. He hurries over to the other car.

Some men in the crowd are extricating the driver. He is bleeding. His eyes are glazed. Somebody calls an ambulance.

Make way for the intern! Fine-looking lad. My, how young!

Here come the cops. Step back there, please. Give the doc a little room.

Examination. Bruises on face; lacerations on forehead; nosebleed. Let's see now. How's this leg? Hmm. Seems

212

okay. Lift your arm, please. That's it. Fine. All right, boys, let's take him along anyway to make sure.

Gangway. Give the man a little air; let the doc through. Okay, Doc, take it away.

Now, who saw this? Anybody see this accident? Don't push, lady; it's all over. They took him away; nobody killed. Anybody see this? What is your name, sir?

"Dribble."

"You tryin' to be funny, mister?"

"What on earth are you talking about, Officer? The name is Dribble and I live at 917 East 64th — "

"All right, all right, don't make a big thing out of it. You actually see this?"

"Actually is right! I nearly got killed myself. That man must think he's a race-track driver, the way he came tearing down — "

"Which man?"

"The one with the goggles; he's still over there by his car, the red convertible, the one with the musical horn there. He was doing sixty, at the least. Not only that, I could tell in a minute — "

"All right, all right, not the story of your life. Save it. Now anybody else here see this accident?"

"Right here, Officer. And it was no accident."

"What!"

"It couldn't have been an accident. I saw the whole thing and it wasn't this man's fault at all, goggles or no goggles. It was the fault of the man they just took away — "

"Bumbel?"

"Whatever his name is. It was his own fault. He was lighting a cigarette at the time — "

"All right, mister, you'll get a chance to tell the whole

213

thing. Now why don't all you people go home? Go to a movie or somethin'! This is all finished — honest! — "

Let's run up to the hospital.

"We want to see Joseph Bumbel, please. Accident case. He was driving a Chevrolet.

"Discharged? Just a few cuts and bruises! Well, that's nice."

Let's look in on Mr. Bumbel at home. The whole family is there.

The Bumbel Home. Evening.

MR. BUMBEL: Yes, sir; sixty miles an hour, and he's coming *against* the light, no less.

MRS. BUMBEL: Oh, I can't bear it! You could have been *killed!* Get your dirty shoes off the couch. You poor dear —

MR. BUMBEL: Now, now. I'm all right. Just a scratch or two. My back, though; my back is a little sore.

MRS. BUMBEL: Joe Bumbel, you'll go to bed this minute! No nonsense, now! You poor —

MR. BUMBEL: Oh, Clara, *please!* I'm all *right.*

MRS. BUMBEL'S BROTHER: Aw, leave him alone; he's all right. Was the guy insured, Joe?

MR. BUMBEL: I don't know; the officers got all the information; I mean his license number and all.

THE BROTHER: You go down and see Frank's lawyer in the morning. We'll see if this guy can do sixty miles an hour against a light!

The Lawyer's Office. Morning.

THE LAWYER: No, Mr. Bumbel, nobody can drive sixty miles an hour against a red light. We'll send him a claim letter right away.

Same Office. One Week Later.

THE LAWYER: Ah, good morning, Mr. Bumbel. Well, he

214

won't settle. He says we're crazy. He says *you* were doing sixty against a red light.

MR. BUMBEL: Look here, that's ridiculous. I *know* I was going slow, and I can prove it. I was lighting a cigarette at the time, and the wind —

THE LAWYER: Mr. Bumbel. Wait. Sit here. This chair is better. Now listen. Carefully. Did I ask you anything about a cigarette?

MR. BUMBEL: No, but —

THE LAWYER: Do you think I'm interested in the wind?

MR. BUMBEL: I'm only trying to prove —

THE LAWYER: Nobody has asked you to *prove* anything, Mr. Bumbel. That's *my* job. Your job is to answer questions. You want to *win* this case, don't you?

MR. BUMBEL: I certainly do! In fact I *must*. My wife is beginning to accuse me of starting the whole thing. In the beginning she was very sympathetic. But then she got to thinking and — you've never met my wife, have you? No, that's right. Well, she's a determined woman. The fact is, I'm getting sick and fed up. One of these days she will be astonished to find —

THE LAWYER: Mr. Bumbel, one case at a time. About this cigarette: everybody smokes; it's nothing new. What's interesting about it? Who wants to know about it? The thing for you to do, from now until the trial, is to stick to the *facts*. Try to remember all the *facts*.

MR. BUMBEL: Well, I *was* lighting this cigarette at the time, and *that's* a fact.

THE LAWYER: Well, it's not the kind of fact *I'm* talking about, and *that's* a fact. Put it this way: You drive a car. You come to a red light. You stop. Well, you answer a question. You come to the end of the answer. You stop. See what I mean? Now let's try it: Were you doing sixty miles an hour on that day?

215

Mr. Bumbel: Why, *no*. Anybody —

The Lawyer: Once more. Try hard, now. Were you doing sixty?

Mr. Bumbel: No.

The Lawyer: Great. I think you'll make it. Now you go home and don't worry about a thing. We'll put the case on the calendar. I'll be in touch with you.

Same Office. One Year Later.

The Lawyer: Ah, good morning, Mr. Bumbel! What can I do for you?

Mr. Bumbel: What can you *do* for me! Where's the trial? It's been a year now —

The Lawyer: Oh, *that*. I can see you're not familiar with these things, Mr. Bumbel. It's only been a year. What you want is patience —

Mr. Bumbel: Wrong. What I want is action. When do you think we'll have a trial? This is ridiculous — to wait a year for a thing —

The Lawyer: Mr. Bumbel, I read character pretty well; I never put you down as a greedy man —

Mr. Bumbel: Listen — lawyer or no lawyer, you're looking for serious trouble! My wife has been after me about this! Have you ever met — no, you haven't. Well, she's been harping on this. She's beginning to accuse me of deliberately putting it off. She says I'm afraid to take the stand.

The Lawyer: Nonsense. Why on earth —

Mr. Bumbel: She says I know I will ball it up the way I do everything else. Anyway, she wants a trial. I mean she's suspicious about the whole thing. Now, I've got to bring back some kind of information tonight. When are we going to have the trial?

The Lawyer: Mr. Bumbel, I sympathize with your position, but these things take time. Why, do you know,

216

a few years ago it took four to six years for a case to be reached —

MR. BUMBEL: Are you out of your mind? My wife won't wait that long. It's out of the question. In fact I think she's already spent part of the money. She's been standing before the mirror lately —

THE LAWYER: I hadn't finished, Mr. Bumbel. The calendar congestion I just mentioned has been greatly improved. I think we have an excellent chance of being reached within a year.

MR. BUMBEL: Another year! Impossible! My —

THE LAWYER: *Within* a year, Mr. Bumbel. It may be a few months. Maybe a month, if we're lucky. Judge Furey has been on the ball lately and is really working like mad. Whenever he has trouble at home he plunges into that court calendar and really makes it move —

MR. BUMBEL: Fantastic! But judge or no judge, we better have a trial real soon. My —

THE LAWYER: I understand perfectly. I'll watch it like a hawk. You'll hear from me soon . . .

Nine Months Later. The Trial.

BUMBEL VS. BROWN! Both sides ready, Your Honor . . . Select your jury, gentlemen . . . Yes, Your Honor . . .

Q: . . . I know this case has taken three days, Your Honor, but I forgot to ask Mr. Bumbel one question. May I recall him at this time?

THE COURT: Certainly, Counselor. One question, you said.

LAWYER: Yes, sir. Mr. Bumbel, you were asked by my learned opponent on cross-examination whether you put out your hand as you approached this intersection. I don't believe I got your answer. Did you?

MR. BUMBEL: *Did* I! Why, like I told the man from the insurance company, the whole —

LAWYER: OBJECT!! I OBJECT!! If Your Honor please,

217

I move for a mistrial! Insurance company . . . Counsel knows better . . . the witness deliberately . . . I move for a mistrial , . . the jury has no right to hear . . . MIS-TRIAL, MISTRIAL, MISTRIAL . . .

Motion granted. Mistrial declared.

Evening. The Bumbel Home.

Mr. Bumbel: All right, all *right*. How was I to know? Am I a lawyer?

Mrs. Bumbel: *Definitely* not.

Six Months Later. New Trial.

Bumbel vs. Brown. Both sides ready, Your Honor . . . Select your jury, gentlemen . . . Yes, Your Honor . . .

. . . And so, ladies and gentlemen, Mr. Bumbel wants to be compensated for his injuries. He does not seek sympathy. He seeks a fair and reasonable sum of money at your hands for his pain and suffering, his excruciating pain and suffering, if you please; for these cuts and bruises and lacerations, and for this sacroiliac sprain. Oh, yes, the young intern didn't find that. He couldn't find it, even if he were an old intern. Mr. Bumbel found it. He found it when he went to bed that night, and he found it every night for seven months, as he testified. You remember his testimony, the tossing and turning, the sleeplessness, and the suffering — these are the things to remember!

Now about this cigarette business, and the so-called eye-witness who calls it to your attention: What do we know about this eyewitness? He is a professional pool-player! Well, really! Are we going to take the word of a pool-player against that of a respectable book-keeper, a family man, a churchgoer? Besides, when I asked him whether the cigarette was lit, he wasn't sure! I think we can all agree that the murky atmo-sphere of a pool hall is not conducive to good eyesight

218

— which would certainly take care of this so-called eyewitness! And remember, Mr. Bumbel swore this cigarette was unlit. I myself am a dry-smoker, and I can understand this. I am constantly fooling with unlighted cigarettes, as you may have noticed. Here is one in my hand now. I think you will agree it has not interfered with my work here —

. . . And now, ladies and gentlemen, we come to this fellow's "injuries." What do they amount to? A bloody nose! And he wants three thousand dollars for it! I am serious, he *does!* Here are the papers! Read them! Why, I would take a bloody nose for a lot less than three thousand dollars! Well, here: Will anybody put a ten-dollar bill on that jury box and give me a bloody nose? Anybody! Anybody at all! Who'll give me ten dollars for a bloody nose . . .

About this cigarette. I *don't* fool with unlighted cigarettes, because I am not *nervous.* If a man is so nervous he needs unlighted cigarettes, I have a question: What is he doing behind the wheel of an automobile! And it has nothing to do with the eyesight of this billiard expert, although if my nervous adversary would care to test the eyesight of our billiardist in a match game for, say, ten dollars, I think we can oblige him. And, while I am not a betting man, I would be inclined to wager the ten I have just been offered for the bloody nose . . .

Twilight, Same Day.

. . . It's hard to say, Mr. Bumbel. Nobody really knows. Sometimes they stay out for hours; sometimes they come right back. Nobody really knows. They've been out three hours, though, which is a good sign . . . *somebody* up there likes our case . . .

219

Later, The Verdict.

Jury ready! Jury ready! Please take seats! Jury ready! . . .
A disagreement!! Well, for the love of heaven!! Well,
really!!

. . . It was that juror in the blue suit . . . didn't like him
from the start . . . and the one with the glasses, he had
a mean look . . . oh, sure, right away . . . the calendar
is in great shape . . . Judge Furey has been working
night and day . . .

Two Months Later.

. . . Select your jury, gentlemen . . . Yes, Your Honor . . .

Twilight.

. . . four hours now . . . good sign . . . here, have one of
mine.

Later.

. . . You say you find a verdict for the plaintiff, Bumbel,
in the sum of one hundred and fifty dollars and so
say you all? . . .

The Lawyer's Office. Three Weeks Later.

Ah, good morning, Mr. Bumbel. Oh, that! . . . Well, they
won't pay. Now, don't get excited . . . have one of
mine . . . they're taking an appeal . . . they claim the
verdict is excessive. Here, you can't do that, Mr. Bumbel; you're carrying this cigarette thing too far; *nobody*
eats cigarettes . . . well, of *course* they won't get away
with it . . . I'm the best appeal man there is. My law
prof — not that door, Mr. Bumbel, that's the broom
closet . . .

Six Months Later.

Good morning, Mr. Bumbel. *I'll* say . . . and it will be
colder tomorrow. Oh, that! Well, it's come back for a
new trial . . . Watch it there! Here, take a shot of this
— do you good . . . Now, here are the minutes of the
last trial. I want you to take them home and read

220

them — cover to cover. The big question on the new trial will be: "Didn't you testify at the last trial" etc., etc. . . . and we don't want any surprises, do we? Now, let's have a little run-through for your general reflexes. The idea is to answer the questions — *only* the questions; no volunteering; no excitement; no bickering; strictly yes or no, and, regardless of the provocation, perfect calm. Ready? Good:

Q: What is your name?

A: Joseph Bumbel.

Q: Do you mean to say that is your real name?

A: Yes.

Q: Ever been convicted of a crime?

A: No.

Q: Are you sure?

A: Yes.

Q: Do you realize you are under oath?

A: Yes.

Q: Do you drink?

A: Yes.

Q: Whisky, I mean.

A: Yes.

Q: Were you ever drunk?

A: Yes.

Q: You *admit* you have been drunk!

A: Yes.

Q: When?

A: Mostly New Year's Eve.

Q: Oh. Are you a heavy smoker?

A: About 148.

Q: Please pay attention. Do you smoke a pack a day?

A: No, sir.

Q: Do you beat your wife?

A: Counselor —

221

Q: Yes?

A: Could I have a glass of water?

Q: Certainly. Here.

A: Thank you.

. . . Mr. Bumbel, you were terrific . . . Now, if you can do that at the trial! . . . But what was that "glass of water" thing? . . .

. . . I was thirsty.

. . . Oh. Well, try to be all set at the trial. We don't want the jury thinking you're stalling . . . but you were great here! . . .

One Month Later.

Jury ready!! . . .

. . . a verdict for the *defendant Brown* and so say you all . . .

. . . Water, please, quickly! Thank you. Now, get hold of yourself, Mr. Bumbel . . . that's better . . . of *course* we'll take an appeal . . . right away . . . you bet . . .

Six Months Later.

. . . a verdict for the *plaintiff Bumbel* in the sum of one hundred seventy-five dollars and so say you all . . .

Three Weeks Later.

THE LAWYER: Ah, good morning, Mr. Bumbel . . . yes, it is . . . ha, ha . . . take this chair here, the soft one . . . ha, ha . . .

MR. BUMBEL: What's so —

THE LAWYER: This is a scream! I can't get over this one! It seems this beautiful broad in an English court was testifying and she was being pretty fresh to the district attorney. Finally the judge said, "Young woman, I suggest you show a little more respect for this gentleman; he's the Crown Solicitor, you know!" And the witness came right back, "Oh, is he indeed, Yur Worship! Well, I'm an 'arf crown solicitor meself, you know!" — Can you *top* that, Bumbel!

MR. BUMBEL: Look, I'm not even going to wait for you to finish that story. Why did you want me to sit in this particular chair? Every time you mention this chair I know —

THE LAWYER: Oh. Yes . . . well . . . Bad news, Mr. Bumbel. *Now you drop that, Mr. Bumbel!* . . . The insurance company that insured Brown has gone broke, sir, and . . . Mr. *Bumbel! Please!! That's an open window, Mr. Bumbel!!* For the love of heaven!!! . . .

It doesn't quite end here. Bumbel is still in the courts and the judges call him Joe. It seems that his nineteen-story leap from the lawyer's window was broken by a stack of pillows left out to air on an eighth-floor ledge by a lawyer addicted to afternoon naps in a French antique chaise longue on this ledge. The antique was ruined by the fall and the lawyer is suing Bumbel for $1500. Bumbel has a counterclaim to this action because of three projecting upholstery nails which he claims had no right to be there.

Meanwhile, Mrs. Bumbel is suing for divorce, on the ground of incompatibility. She claims that since these trials Bumbel has become so adroit under cross-examination there is no living with him; he has an answer for any situation and is quite insufferable.

Her brother is suing Bumbel's original lawyer for malpractice, alleging that instead of watching the calendar like a hawk, he should have been watching the insurance company like an eagle. This brother threatens to take it to the highest court because if the home breaks up he has no place to go, and he cannot work — it makes him nervous.

The lawyer on the eighth floor is suing the landlord of the building on the ground that Bumbel was the third client to come through that window within a month and that the landlord should have known about the danger and taken the necessary measures.

Judge Furey is well out of it. He tripped in a toe-trap on the courthouse steps during the third trial of Bumbel's second case and is in the hospital, but he threatens to —

Well, actually there *is* no end.

About the Author

ALEXANDER ROSE's *expert understanding of every variety of court behavior from stuttering denial to bland confession of guilt comes from the more than twenty years he spent as Official Court Reporter in courts ranging from New York Magistrates to the United States District Court.*

He lists "Tinkerer" as his non-writing occupation and can produce papers from the U.S. Patent Office to prove it. Among his inventions are the Typatune ("a musical instrument," Mr. Rose explains, "with a typewriter keyboard"); the Ev-A-Strate Picture Hanger ("crooked pictures a thing of the past"); and an additional invention he calls The World's Greatest Toothpick ("shaped like a very small golf club"), which he has marketed successfully across the country. He has written a weekly newspaper column called "Ring Around the Rose," plays the accordion, travels to Europe as often as not, and lives today in New York City with his family.

225